American Mosaic

American Mosaic

AFRICAN-AMERICAN CONTRIBUTIONS

The History of Jazz

Sandy Asirvatham

CHELSEA HOUSE
PUBLISHERS

A Haights Cross Communications Company

Philadelphia

Frontis: A set of stamps issued by the United States Postal Service commemorating legends of jazz, underscores jazz's undeniable significance to American culture.

CHELSEA HOUSE PUBLISHERS

VP, New Product Development Sally Cheney
Director of Production Kim Shinners
Creative Manager Takeshi Takahashi
Manufacturing Manager Diann Grasse

Staff for THE HISTORY OF JAZZ

Associate Editor Benjamin Xavier Kim
Production Editor Jaimie Winkler
Photo Editor Sarah Bloom
Cover and Series Designer Keith Trego
Layout 21st Century Publishing and Communications, Inc.

A Haights Cross Communications ✦ Company

http://www.chelseahouse.com

First Printing

1 3 5 7 9 8 6 4 2

Library of Congress Cataloging-in-Publication Data

Asirvatham, Sandy.
  The history of jazz/Sandy Asirvatham.
    p. cm.—(American mosaic)
Includes index.
  ISBN 0-7910-7265-7HC   0-7910-7489-7PB
  1. Jazz—History and criticism—Juvenile literature.
[1. Jazz. 2. African American music—History and criticism.]
I. Title. II. Series.
NL3506 .A75 2003
781.65'089'96073—dc21

                                    2002154355

Table of Contents

Vibraphonist Lionel Hampton, left, and clarinetist Benny Goodman, right, were pioneering bandleaders during jazz's big band era. Lionel Hampton first joined Benny Goodman's band in the 1930s during a time when players of different races did not integrate onstage, and jazz was still finding its identity.

The Color
of Jazz

The various musical styles that travel under the label "jazz" have always generated controversy among musicians and music audiences. Even the label itself has been continually scrutinized, debated, and redefined. To this day, players, fans, historians, and journalists are still trying to determine what jazz is—what kinds of sounds count as "real" jazz.

Since it originated in the particular experiences of African Americans struggling to live decently in an often hostile, white-dominated society, jazz has been a source of debate and difference between blacks and whites. In the 1920s, for example, white classical musicians and devotees were apt to think of jazz as primitive, savage, unrefined, or degenerate—the same negative qualities generally used to stereotype African-American people. And yet jazz has experienced the same strange transformation of so many African-based musical styles in this country, such as blues and rap: a journey from the margins to the very center of American musical culture.

Although invented by a minority population living outside the

political, economic, and cultural mainstream, jazz at its few
moments of great popularity became an element in the kinds of
music that nearly all Americans preferred to listen to and purchase.
Within a few decades of its invention, jazz came to be revered by
at least some core audience as both an enjoyable "popular" music
and a sophisticated "art" music all around the world—one of
this nation's most successful and influential cultural exports.

Since blacks in this country do not constitute—and have never
constituted—a monolithic, single-minded community enjoying
perfect solidarity, jazz music has also been a long-standing source
of contention and difference among African Americans themselves. Middle-class blacks in the early and middle part of the
20th century, for example, were apt to distance themselves from
jazz music, associating it with what they took to be the crime- and
sin-filled lifestyle of its "lower-class" musicians and fans.

There have always been generational as well as class differences
in the response to jazz. In the 1920s, a writer for *The Ladies' Home
Journal* blamed the syncopated rhythms of jazz for demoralizing
and corrupting young men and women—and in doing so, she
simultaneously echoed complaints about ragtime and other older
popular music forms, and anticipated later criticisms about rock
and roll, heavy metal, and rap. Today's African-American youths,
in contrast, have no reason to question the "respectability" of
jazz, a once-rebellious, now-established music their parents and
grandparents may love; but younger people may prefer to listen to
hip-hop and other genres that evoke the subversive, the aggressive,
and even the criminal aspects of life. As has long been the
case, one generation's musical rebellion often becomes the next
generation's mainstream.

While these ongoing social controversies swirl around "outside"
the music, there have always been conflicts among "insiders" as
well, particularly when it comes to defining the sonic boundaries of
the term "jazz" itself. Like its close cousin the blues, jazz can be seen
as both young—a phenomenon of the 20th century—and very
old—originating not just in the 17th and 18th century slave trade

but in the indigenous religious and musical practices of native Africans dating back thousands of years. The blues has sprouted offshoots and hybrids—most notably, guitar-based rock and roll—but generally remains a singular and recognizable musical sound. A modern blues fan, for example, can point to a number of features that help define a song as "the blues" or at least "bluesy": the ubiquitous 12-bar format, the tonic-subdominant-dominant harmonic structure, the use of "bent" or "blue" notes (tones that don't appear on or fall between the notes of traditional Western scales), the prevalence of electric guitars and harmonicas, the recurrence of certain traditional themes and patterns in the lyrics.

Jazz, in contrast, contains so many different kinds of sounds today that it is almost impossible to summarize and define. A local "jazz band" today—playing for, say, an only slightly attentive audience during brunch at a restaurant—may offer a hugely varied repertoire of song styles from different eras: bossa nova rhythms from the 1960s, big band swing tunes from the 1930s or 1940s, fast and furious bebop melodies from the late 1940s, Beatles rock tunes revamped to include improvised solos, pop or funk numbers from the 1970s, and others. The members of that jazz band may laugh when the maitre d' comes up to them between sets and innocently asks to hear "something jazzy," but they won't be surprised. Since musicians themselves debate the meaning of the word, they know not to expect non-musicians to fully understand it. Even musicians who play in other styles—modern symphonic or "classical" music, for example—often have very little concept of what jazz is.

In his introductory college textbook *Jazz Styles: History and Analysis*, author Mark C. Gridley begins his first chapter as follows and demonstrates just how difficult it is to define this music:

> Jazz includes many different streams of music. They can be played by almost any combination of instruments. They can evoke almost any mood. Some are light and happy. Some are heavy and serious. Some make you want to dance. Some make you think. Some are

smooth and predictable. Some are agitated and full of surprises. Jazz can be heard in many different places. It is often presented as serious music in concert halls. Some jazz is played in ballrooms for dancers. There is jazz in background music on the radio. Much jazz is played in night clubs where people listen while they drink and talk with their friends.

Such a "definition" reads almost like a newspaper horoscope: it is so open to interpretation that it can mean almost anything to anyone. Thus, to try to differentiate jazz from other kinds of music, Gridley points to its two most significant features: "its provocative rhythms and . . . its insistence that performers create their parts as they play them."

To be sure, these two features are present in other musical genres as well. Many of the rhythmic conventions underlying jazz are essentially holdovers from African culture, but those same conventions were brought by slaves to many parts of North and South America and the Caribbean, and ultimately played an important part in the development of almost all popular musical styles from these regions, including the blues, salsa, calypso, reggae, rock, hip-hop, and numerous others. And even improvisation—the "insistence that performers create their parts as they play them"—has some limited role in other forms of American popular music, particularly blues and bluegrass.

For devoted jazz fans, however, improvisation is often the name of the game, the entire point of the music. As Gridley writes:

Hearing live jazz is exciting not only for the way it makes us feel but also for the realization that we are following the musical thinking of the musicians at the very moment they are inventing their music. They are taking us along with them while they make up fresh sounds. This is akin to the impossible situation of seeing a finished painting as we watch the artist apply paint to the canvas, *at the same time* as we watch one manufacturer produce the canvas and another manufacturer produce the paints themselves.

People dancing at London's Jazz Club in 1949 to jazz—just one of the many ways that the music can be enjoyed even in places far outside of its birthplace.

As we will see in the next chapter and throughout this book, Americans of African heritage—whether this means "pure" black ancestry or "mixed"—were overwhelmingly responsible for the creation and early development of Dixieland music, the precursor to modern jazz. In the middle of the 20th century, the greatest innovators and originators of various historical jazz styles were, with rare exception, black American men: Louis Armstrong, Duke Ellington, Count Basie, Lester Young, Charlie Parker, John Coltrane, Miles Davis, and others. Musicians of non-African ethnic backgrounds—such as trumpeter Bix Beiderbecke and clarinetist Benny Goodman during the swing era, or pianist

Bill Evans later on, among several others—have made significant contributions to its development, but there are some historians who believe that, due to a kind of "reverse discrimination," these white players have generally not received enough credit from listeners and historians. Even if that is true, however, it is safe to assume that, without the unique history of the North Atlantic Slave Trade and the presence of a significant population of blacks in a white-dominated society, there would be no jazz today.

Yet to call jazz "black music" or "African-American music"—to try to put both cultural and aesthetic boundaries around it by referring to a racial category—does not simplify the task of defining what jazz is. Jazz writers have traditionally said that although the harmonic and melodic contents of jazz derive from Western sources (e.g., European "classical" music of the 19th century), the defining feature of jazz—what makes it a distinctive style—is its African-based rhythmic sensibility. This view, while not wholly inaccurate, is now thought to be an oversimplification. As composer and author Gunther Schuller wrote in his classic 1968 history *Early Jazz: Its Roots and Musical Development*, a close study of jazz's antecedents shows that its "African and European lineages [are] somewhat entangled, as is inevitable in . . . a hybrid that evolved through many stages of cross-fertilization over a period of more than a century."

Still, Schuller and others acknowledge the close cultural and philosophical relationship between native African music and early American jazz, for

both originate in a total vision of life, in which music, unlike the "art music" of Europe, is not a separate, autonomous social domain. African music, like its sister arts—sculpture, mural drawing, and so forth—is conditioned by the same stimuli that animate not only African philosophy and religion, but the entire social structure. In so far as it has not been influenced by European or American customs, African music even today has no separate abstracted function.

To put the matter more simply, art is not separate from religion, and religion is not separate from daily life in the African tradition. Music is, like all other creative forms, functional rather than decorative—a necessary element in the lives of individuals and communities. "It not surprising that the word 'art' does not even exist in African languages," Schuller notes. "Nor does the African divide art into separate categories. Folklore, music, dance, sculpture, and painting operate as a total generic unit, serving not only religion but all phases of daily life, encompassing birth, death, work, and play."

Furthermore, African music shares a closer relationship with spoken language than it does in the European and American traditions. "Basically," writes Schuller, "language functions only in conjunction with rhythm. All verbal activity . . . is rhythmicized. And it is no mere coincidence that the languages and dialects of the African Negro are in themselves a form of music, often to the extent that certain syllables possess specific intensities, durations, and even pitch levels." Thus, scholars see connections between the musical richness of African languages and some of the traditions of American jazz, such as the practice of scatting (singing improvised lines that imitate the sound of instruments) or the technique of using certain instruments, such as trombones or drums, to imitate the sound of words.

So there are ways in which jazz is undeniably and very profoundly rooted in the African parts of its heritage. And yet, labeling jazz "black music" can lead to loaded questions and further debates. As Gridley, Schuller, and other historians point out, jazz was born in New Orleans—a racially complex society where French, Spanish, and African musical influences intermingled freely, making it impossible to trace "pure" African or "pure" European elements in the music. Furthermore, although the musical framework created by the early jazz musicians—the common practices and concepts that went into a typical jazz performance—came out of the specific culture of a certain group of black Americans at the turn of the 20th century, this framework or set of practices was so powerful and so flexible that it came to be imitated, learned, assimilated, and ultimately transformed by members of other cultural groups. White Americans made use of jazz in this way, but then so did Europeans, Japanese, Indians, and others all over the world.

At the heart of much jazz, for example, is the idea of taking a popular song, perhaps even a very simple and insubstantial one, and using it as a "vehicle" to create sophisticated, exciting, on-the-spot embellishments or variations on the song's theme. Taking their cue from American jazz musicians—who might use vaudeville numbers, or Broadway show tunes, or popular folk songs as the basis for jazz renditions—musicians all over the world have been inspired to mine their own culture's musical heritage and to turn familiar songs into vehicles for improvisation. The resulting sounds might bear very little resemblance to the sounds of what people commonly think of as traditional, African-American jazz. Some people would have no trouble calling these sounds jazz because they are rooted in jazz practices. Others would resist applying the label to something so seemingly different.

Jazz history continues to be dogged by such differences of opinion. As a simple matter of fact, jazz has become a universal music; literally anyone of any racial or ethnic origin is free to try to play it. Yet there persists a notion that the music is less "authentically" jazz if white Americans or members of other non-African ethnic groups play it. This idea may be connected to the concept—held by some scientists and non-scientists alike—that cultural preferences are biologically inherited rather than learned. Gridley, for one, explicitly rejects this kind of thinking:

When African-American ragtime and blues began affecting the performance of other kinds of music, some observers contended that the race of the musician was responsible for the particular way the music was played. For example, many listeners felt that the highly rhythmic nature of African-American forms reflected a rhythmic talent that came with the race of the musician.

Historians note that many features of jazz are African in origin and were brought to the New World by slaves. This fact has helped fuel the notion that blacks are naturally better at playing jazz than whites—a loaded racial concept that is still debated today.

Preferences for certain African techniques were indeed passed down from generation to generation by imitation and instruction. But slaves also learned European music that was available . . . it is not reasonable to expect all music played by blacks to sound African. No one inherits desires for music of any particular region; there is no "racial unconscious" that is transmitted genetically.

Although mainstream American society has come a long way from the blatant segregationist thinking of the early part of this century, racially divisive questions still circulate among us. In terms of jazz specifically, some people still ask whether non-black musicians are capable of playing jazz as well as their African-American counterparts—whether they can sound as good, or as "real," if they didn't grow up experiencing life as a black person in this culture. Others contend that they can tell the race of a musician just by hearing him or her play and noting the presence or absence of certain stylistic conventions rooted in African-American culture. Trumpeter Roy Eldridge, an African American, once told Bruce Lundvall, president of the famous recording label Blue Note Records, that he could always tell if a musician was black or white based on sound alone. But Lundvall (who is white) then gave Eldridge a "blindfold test," playing various records for him and asking him to identify the race of the musicians. The trumpeter, Lundvall says, was wrong about 60 percent of time.

In other instances, people have questioned the authenticity or genuineness of certain hybrid forms of music that emerged out of different cultural circumstances in other countries—for example, Brazilian bossa nova, or the various Latin jazz styles invented by New York musicians of Cuban, Dominican, and Puerto Rican descent. Since they are not specifically African-American, are these "really jazz"? What about the jazz-funk and jazz-rock fusions of the 1970s and 1980s? What about the "smooth jazz" sounds of Kenny G? Do these count as the "real deal"?

Jazz observers also sometimes wonder what to make of the fact that the vast majority of jazz fans, record buyers, educators, and musicians are white rather than black (though this is a matter of raw numbers rather than relative percentages: for example, recent studies show that African Americans make up only 11 percent of the American population but up to 20 percent of all jazz audience members). Indeed, by some measures, jazz is more beloved outside of America than inside. In a magazine interview in the summer of 2002, Canadian-born pianist Renee Rosnes noted that Europeans, for example, generally respect the music much more than do Americans—a fact all touring jazz musicians know well:

> In general, there's more appreciation of culture [in Europe]. I just got back from Germany, and it's a great example. We performed at the jazz institute . . . and the people who run it gave each of us a thick hard-covered book that we could keep. It lists all of the jazz clubs and concert promoters . . . in Germany. It's *huge*! Every little town has an event presented sometime in the year. It's totally amazing. You couldn't begin to have a book like that in America . . .

Here in the country of jazz's birthplace, some people are happy to celebrate the simple fact that this music still retains a fiercely loyal core audience—albeit a very tiny minority among all music lovers worldwide. Yet others are tempted to believe that when jazz lost its fundamental, almost exclusive connection to African-American musicians and listeners, it also lost its soul.

These many thorny issues about race, culture, and "authenticity" are well beyond the scope of this brief history. But as you read through the following pages, perhaps you will start to formulate some of your own ideas about these and other issues, or to ask questions of your own.

On one level, jazz is just like any other kind of music: it exists simply to be played, danced to, listened to, rejoiced in. On another level, jazz is a cultural phenomenon with a fascinating, complicated, contentious history that connects with larger philosophical issues of heritage and identity in America. We will try to touch on both these aspects of jazz—the "purely" musical, and the social or philosophical—in what follows.

New Orleans, Louisiana is seen as the birthplace of jazz. It was here in the early 1900s where Hispanic, African, and French influences mixed and gave rise to the unique Creole heritage.

2

The Crucible of
New Orleans

By the end of the 19th century, just a few generations beyond the Emancipation Proclamation and the abolition of slavery, black Americans all around the country had already developed an extensive musical culture that hosted both professionals and amateurs playing a wide variety of styles. In a very broad and general sense, this musical culture blended practices of African origin—such as "call and response" singing, or the combination of various rhythmic patterns into complex "polyrhythms"—with the European-based melodic and harmonic resources that blacks absorbed from the world around them, most notably from Christian church music. This blending was not a conscious or deliberate set of actions, but a slow and unintentional (and inevitable) process that arose when two very different traditions lived side-by-side in the New World.

In the Mississippi Delta and other parts of the Deep South, cotton plantation workers with musical gifts were beginning to develop a unique style of guitar-playing and singing that would come to be known as the blues. In Negro colleges around the country, all-black choral groups were singing music by European and white American composers, adding their own expressive, gospel-music flavor to standard works. In the burgeoning circuit of black vaudeville theaters around the country, singers and dancers were developing homegrown forms of entertainment that their fellow African Americans would particularly relate to and enjoy.

But jazz had a separate development from many of these black folk-music styles because it originated in the unique racial heritage of New Orleans, Louisiana—a mix of Hispanic, French, and African historical influences that set this society apart from the rest of the New World. In the 18th century, the Louisiana territory alternated between French and Spanish rule, and it ultimately inherited customs and cultural habits from both cultures. Although slaves from Africa were present as early as 1719, there were also free blacks living in New Orleans as early as 1722. Under Spanish rule in the middle of the century, marriage between New Orleans citizens of different ethnic descent was not uncommon. Eventually, the children of these mixed marriages came to be known as Creoles: "Creoles of Color" were those with part-African, part-French ancestry, while "white Creoles" were the offspring of mixed French-Spanish heritage.

The Creoles of Color eventually came to be seen—and to see themselves—as a separate class. For a time, their social status generally made them closer to whites than to either slaves or free Negroes who had little or no white ancestry. Later on during the 19th century, a series of social and legal changes gradually eroded the Creoles' separate echelon. As "pure" whites came to regard anybody with any African blood as "black," Creoles and Negroes were consigned to the same low status. New Orleans' unique racial mix generated a complex social hierarchy that continues to play a role in the city's society and politics even today.

Stuck halfway between low-status Negroes and high-status whites, ambitious members of 19th-century Creole society were generally interested in distancing themselves from the African part of their ancestry. Well-educated and often well-to-do, Creoles tended to live downtown in what is now called the French quarter, and their musical tastes were highly refined. They frequented the city's three opera houses and obtained high-quality, Parisian-style musical education for their children. While the downtown Creoles of Color grew up with the sounds of European concert-hall music, the less wealthy residents of uptown—those identified as Negroes—developed a sound derived from African-American work songs and field hollers which were inherited from their slave parents and grandparents. These musicians were often formally untrained, and grew up learning music "by ear," often developing fantastic listening and imitative skills as a result.

From the beginning, there were cross-cultural influences between these two social groups. Ragtime music, a very popular style in the late 1800s, borrowed from military marches and from African-American banjo music. While the harmonic and melodic elements were European in origin, the ragtime practice of syncopation—that is, of putting accents on weak beats, where they are not normally expected—had African roots. Ragtime syncopation ultimately became the precursor of one of jazz's defining characteristics: the concept of swing rhythm or swing feel. Swing has proven very difficult to define in musical terms, although Gridley does a fairly good job:

> One of the easily defined factors causing swing feeling is *constant tempo*. This helps us distinguish it from kinds of symphonic music where conductors are free to vary the tempo

while playing a piece. A steady beat is nearly always kept in jazz pieces. It brings a certain momentum that is essential to swing feeling. Much of the excitement in jazz comes for musicians in the band tugging against this very solid foundation by playing notes slightly before or after the beat.

Gridley also mentions the cohesive, precisely synchronized group sound and the rhythmic lilt that contribute to swing feeling. He writes, "The different members need not be playing the same rhythms in unison, but each player must execute the rhythms of his part with great precision in relation to beat and the sounds of the other instruments. The group cannot swing if its members are not playing closely together."

New Orleans at this time was a lively, cosmopolitan seaport— a center of commerce for America and for the world filled with tourists and travelers. Music was everywhere—in taverns, dance halls, and houses of prostitution, and right out on the street during frequent parades. People wanted to get up and dance to the music rather than sit and listen, and both Creole and black musicians became adept at playing European dance styles such as mazurkas, waltzes, and quadrilles. In the search for new, more exciting sounds to please their audiences, they also began combining influences—adding ragtime syncopations to traditionally non-syncopated dances, for example. Thus, musicians were constantly pushed to stretch their imaginations and their musical resources to come up with fresh, crowd-pleasing sounds. In this hectic musical marketplace, brass bands and string bands had to be quick and adaptable. Their flexible style came to known as "Dixieland." Gridley describes the genesis of this form:

In parades as well as dance halls, small bands were trying to perform music originally written for large bands . . . In trying to fill out the sound, more activity was required of each player, so

A form of music known as "Dixieland" was the predecessor to jazz, employing improvisation and adaptability in order to keep crowds happy and dancing. European dance styles were infused with other influences, such as ragtime, and bands came up with new arrangements to fit their particular ensembles' instrumentation.

musicians improvised parts to order. They got in the habit of improvising, and, as jazz evolved, this habit changed from a necessity into a choice.

Improvisation was, according to Gridley, a well-established practice in America by this time, in both the formal repertoire—e.g., European concert music, where improvised ornaments and cadenzas had always been common—and in folk music. Still, though, as "Dixieland" slowly gave birth to early jazz, improvisation came to be more important to a performance than the original tune itself. "This trend evolved across the 1920s," writes Gridley, "and in some performances of the 1930s all that remained of the original was the tune's spirit and chord progressions. What we call improvisation, early musicians referred to as 'messin' around,' embellishing, 'jassing,' or 'jassing up.'"

As previously mentioned, Dixieland bands playing popular dance music often had to accommodate themselves to scores or arrangements written for larger ensembles. When first rehearsing or performing these published musical pieces, musicians might improvise sections on the spot in order to make all the various sections come together or to fill in for missing instruments. Writes Gridley of the improvisations:

> Trombone counterlines, clarinet obbligatos, and trumpet variations of the melody were sometimes invented and performed spontaneously. Accompaniments [e.g., by rhythm section players such as pianists] were improvised and varied by the more adventurous and creative players. After a suitable set of parts had been worked out, the musicians frequently remained relatively loyal to them. The extent to which new melodies were freshly improvised during performance was limited. There was, however, a striving for personalization and individualization . . .

"By the late 1920s, these improvisational tendencies had expanded to the extent of improvisation we usually expect from most jazz today," Gridley writes. "Unfortunately, we do not know why this change occurred." We do, however, know the names and something of the biographies of the most important and influential artists of this period—the great geniuses of early jazz improvisation.

King Oliver's Dixie Syncopators were one of the bands started by Joe "King" Oliver, a New Orleans transplant to Chicago, in the 1920s. He also started the Creole Jazz Band, which employed a young Louis Armstrong, who would take solo improvisation to a new level with his unique approach to the trumpet.

3

A Soloist's Art

We do not really know what turn-of-the-century New Orleans music sounded like, as there are almost no recordings of it. As Gridley notes, "what is usually referred to as New Orleans style is not the music that was played between 1910 and 1920 in New Orleans . . . but rather the music recorded by New Orleans musicians in Chicago during the 1920s." These musicians were among the hundreds of thousands of African Americans who migrated in this period from rural Dixie to the northern industrial cities—primarily New York and Chicago—hoping to escape the overt racial discrimination of the Jim Crow South and to find good-paying jobs.

Our concepts of Dixieland and early jazz come mostly from written observations made at the time and later interviews with players still living into the middle of the 20th century. Scholars agree that early jazz generally featured collective improvisation, in which all the various instrumentalists would spontaneously create phrases and lines to complement each other and build a group sound. But a few extremely innovative individual musicians—most notably, Louis Armstrong, Bix Beiderbecke, and Sidney Bechet—helped transform this music from a mostly collective endeavor into a forum for the highest, most imaginative forms of soloist expression. These soloing geniuses turned what was once a team sport into something akin to baseball: a game that features distinctive individual efforts against the backdrop of group play.

In the early 1920s, a New Orleans transplant in Chicago named Joe "King" Oliver formed his famous Creole Jazz Band, which played regularly in the city's South Side. In Schuller's words, the Creole Jazz Band "represents the New Orleans style's last-ditch stand before the world and at the same time its finest full flowering." Oliver's band was pure Dixieland-style jazz in "its joy, its warmth of expression, its Old World pre-war charm, its polyphonic complexity, its easy relaxed swing, as heady as a hot summer night in New Orleans, its lovely instrumental textures, and its discipline and logic." Oliver himself played the cornet, an early type of trumpet, and was well respected for it, but his playing paled in comparison with that of his newly hired young protégé. Schuller writes that "Louis Armstrong, 15 years younger than his mentor, was to . . . precipitate the first major revolution in jazz."

The son of a New Orleans prostitute and a childhood truant and troublemaker, young Armstrong would eventually become an international star. His earliest recordings, such as his performance on the King Oliver composition "West End Blues," are still revered as classics, as are his 1927 sessions with the bands he led, the Hot Five and the Hot Seven. Blessed with a full, bright tone and the large, powerful range, Armstrong brought a whole new conception to jazz instrumental playing. "He'd shorten some notes, length and others, and loosen up the rhythm until the music began to ebb and flow instead of following the rigid rocking ragtime," according to Ron David, author of *Jazz for Beginners*. "He built his improvisations like songs within a song, and his trumpet sound glowed." As Gridley puts it, Armstrong "calmly forged sensible lines that had both the flow of spontaneity and the stamp of finality. His improvisations [were] well-paced, economical statements. The organization of Armstrong's phrases [suggested] that he was thinking ahead, yet the phrases [managed] to sound spontaneous rather than calculated."

Other improvisers during this period tended to simply embellish or paraphrase the tune's melody. Armstrong could certainly do this sort of thing, but he became a master at creating original new melodies based upon the underlying harmonic structure of the composition. In a later chapter, we will also explore how Armstrong's gruff-voiced, distinctive singing style and scatting technique came to influence popular singers for generations to come.

Another noteworthy trumpeter of this era was Bix Beiderbecke, a young contemporary of Armstrong's. Although he died before he reached the age of 30 from pneumonia and the ravages of alcoholism, Beiderbecke achieved great and lasting fame as the featured soloist for the Paul Whiteman Orchestra. The wide-ranging historical influence of Beiderbecke—a white Midwesterner from Davenport, Iowa—certainly complicates the image of jazz as an exclusively African-American music. Gridley describes the contrast between the styles of Beiderbecke and Armstrong:

> Beiderbecke was almost as original and creative as Armstrong, but he had less command over his instrument and a bit cooler sound. Beiderbecke's tone was softer, lighter weight, and less brassy than Armstrong's. His rhythmic approach was less aggressive. Like most early jazz players, he did not have pronounced jazz swing feeling when he began performing, but later he developed a swing feeling which approached that of Armstrong . . . he was less dramatic and more subtle. In contrast to Armstrong's assured, outgoing style, Beiderbecke was quieter and considerably more restrained. He played more in the instrument's middle register than did Armstrong, who liked high notes. Beiderbecke also pays more attention to stringing together unusual note choices and acknowledging every passing chord in the progression—something he knew well because he was also a good pianist.

Another pioneering jazz soloist was trumpeter Bix Beiderbecke, who hailed from Davenport, Iowa. His playing style was subtler and more restrained than that of his contemporary, Louis Armstrong.

Clarinetist and soprano saxophonist Sidney Bechet, a New Orleans native of Creole background, was another of the first important jazz soloists. Like Armstrong, he had a fantastic, natural sense of solo structure, and was able to create dazzling, on-the-spot improvisations that seemed like prepared compositions. He also had an instinctive sense of swing. Some historians liken his playing to the earthy, funky singing style of blues vocalists. He liked to scoop or smear notes, approaching the pitch from above or below and delaying the arrival of notes for maximum dramatic effect—a technique that became standard for jazz horn players.

These three soloists were among the most influential of a whole generation of musicians who created the early jazz sound. Among piano players, James P. Johnson was among the first to transition from ragtime playing to jazz, by replacing the stiff, march-like stride style with a more fluid approach. Pianists Earl Hines and Jelly Roll Morton also had far-reaching influence. Johnny Dodds and Jimmie Noone were noteworthy clarinetists of this early jazz period, while Jack Teagarden—a white Texan—and New Orleans native Kid Ory were prominent experts on the trombone, arguably the most difficult of brass instruments to master.

The rhythm section players—which might include guitarists, banjo players, tuba players, string bassists, pianists, and drummers—were generally not very innovative in this era, and played a primarily supportive role for the stars and journeymen among the frontline horn players. Not until the bebop era of the late 1940s and 1950s would rhythm section players assert a more prominent role for themselves as both collective improvisers and soloists.

A much-noted irony of early jazz history is that the first Dixieland-style recording was made by a group of white, rather than black, musicians. The Original Dixieland Jazz Band, led by cornet player Nick LaRocca, recorded its first 78 rpm album in 1917, with "Livery Stable Blues" on the A-side and "Dixie Jazz Band One-Step" on the B-side. It was a hugely successful record. In 1923, King Oliver's Creole Jazz Band made several sides often thought to be the first recordings by a black New Orleans combo. Another New Orleans band combo belonging to trombonist Kid Ory, however, was actually the first black combo to have its music issued on record a few years earlier than that.

In his textbook, Gridley separates the Chicago jazz scene of the 1920s into three categories: black musicians from New Orleans, white musicians from New Orleans, and young white Chicago natives who were influenced by both white and black Dixieland players and who developed a more frenetic, aggressive form of early jazz that came to be called the Chicago style or school. New York City was not yet a hotbed of jazz innovation and recording, though it would eventually become nothing less than the international capital of jazz.

Looked at more closely, the fact that an all-white band was the first to record jazz is not really much of a paradox given the larger historical context of American race relations. The social and professional circles of musicians were, in most cases, just as racially segregated and hierarchical as American society overall. Jazz came from black culture but was introduced to mainstream America through white musicians. Some of these men were great musicians in their own right, while others were less-skilled imitators. (At the same time, however, it would be wrong to assume that all black musicians of this era, or any other, were capable of playing jazz well.) In *Jazz for Beginners*, author Ron David notes with an understandable sense of frustration and more than a little sarcasm,

> The Original Dixieland Jazz Dand got the credit, money, and fame. Paul Whiteman was the King of Jazz, [clarinetist] Benny Goodman was the king of swing, Hollywood made nice movies about Bix Beiderbecke, Benny Goodman, Glenn Miller, the Dorsey brothers, Red Nichols, and other [white] "Jazz Greats." And when bands were finally integrated, black musicians often couldn't eat in the same restaurants, sleep in the same hotels, or [use the same bathrooms] as their palefaced brothers—but at least they were paid a lot less money than the white guys!

In jazz, the belief that white musicians were exploitative "pretenders" coexists with the opposite—and possibly quite nostalgic and inaccurate—belief that among musicians, even in the Jim Crow era, the only thing that mattered was whether you could play well. Louis and Bix, for example, played with each other, respected each other, and learned from each other. Racial optimists tend to rely on the exhilarating accounts of white musicians and fans defying their own cultural norms by traveling to black neighborhood clubs to play and listen to jazz. Such musicians are often seen as brave individuals who were able to forge relationships that transcended the entrenched American habits of racial separation and hostility.

But more pessimistic and less romantically inclined observers are not willing to paint a picture of racial utopia among jazz musicians as a whole, in this era or any other. They see the unequal structures of the larger society clearly reflected among musicians. For example, they may point to the fact that in many genres of American music, some white record producers have profited handsomely from black musical styles while cheating the artists themselves out of their fair share, while some white musicians have grown internationally famous playing songs written by obscure, penniless African Americans. There will probably always be a divide between these optimists and pessimists—those who focus on moments of racial cooperation and harmony in jazz, versus those who see nothing but a continuation of the racial strife that existed in all of American society.

Ella Fitzgerald, one of America's greatest singers in any style, sang with many big bands and gained fame along with fellow singers like Louis Prima and Frank Sinatra during the 1930s and 1940s—what is now called the "golden age of jazz," when swing music's popularity was at its all-time high.

Hot Swing, Sweet Swing

The swing or Big Band era of the 1930s and 1940s is commonly thought of as the "golden" era of jazz, when the music reached the zenith of its popularity. But this generalized historical notion is, like so many statements about jazz, a bit of an oversimplification. Gridley breaks down the idea as follows:

> If music can be called jazz solely by its association with the jazz tradition, the swing era was a great period for jazz. And if music can be called jazz whenever it swings, this era clearly marks a peak for jazz. But if we employ a strict definition and require jazz to be improvised, the matter becomes sticky.

During this time period, large dance bands employing as many as 16 musicians grew to be hugely popular across the nation, among both blacks and whites of many ages and social classes. But different bands emphasized different things. Some of them presented heavily crafted orchestrations with little or no room for improvisation, while others focused very strongly on the soloing skills of its star players. Some bands could be considered "swinging" while others had a more "square" rhythmic feel, akin to formal concert-hall music.

The fact that all big band music was not associated with jazz is still evident today: people who were teenagers or young adults in the '30s and '40s, for example, often consider "big band" and "jazz" to be two totally separate categories of music, with the word "jazz" signifying later styles of music, such as bebop, that aren't suitable for dancing. Furthermore, almost all styles of later jazz — bebop, cool, avant-garde, Latin jazz, and so on — have spawned important large-format bands, consisting of 10 or more pieces. Even today at the start of the 21st century, certain cities like New York and London are home to several influential large jazz bands. But the sounds these groups create do not always fall under the aesthetic category of "swing" or "big band" music.

It must also be recognized that many of the most popular swing era bands featured beloved vocalists such as Louis Prima, Ella Fitzgerald, and Frank Sinatra doing renditions of previously familiar songs. Gridley and other historians have thus noted that the apparent popularity of jazz in this time period was, in reality, simply a reflection of the perennial popularity of dance and vocal music, whatever the genre:

> Jazz historians, being jazz fans themselves, like to believe that the adulation of the swing big bands was directed mostly at jazz qualities of the music. It is more likely however, that most fans were more entranced by the overall effect of big band music than by the inspiration and skill with which solo improvisers devised their lines.

But even if jazz improvisation was merely incidental to the

popularity of big band music, this era was an important, formative one for the jazz that came after it. Most of the jazz giants of the late 1940 and early 1950s cut their teeth playing swing music, and some of them continued to play in large-format ensembles for decades after the swing era.

Swing bands of the '30s and '40s were often characterized as either being "sweet" or "hot." Sweet bands featured lush arrangements and emphasized vocal numbers rather than instrumentals; they were typically led and staffed by white musicians. Glenn Miller and Tommy Dorsey headed up two of the most popular such bands. But the big bands that were most important to the later development of modern jazz were "hot" ones, and were generally (though not exclusively) associated with African-American musicians.

Many of the great early improvisers worked with bandleader Fletcher Henderson between the early 1920s and mid-1930s. Henderson and his arranger, Don Redman, helped define the rhythmic conventions that gave the band a sure and steady sense of swing; they were aided in this task by the indomitable Louis Armstrong, who became Henderson's chief soloist in 1924.

Benny Goodman, a master clarinetist, was one of the few white musicians to lead a very jazz-oriented, hard-driving, hot band—and also one of the few ensemble leaders who hired both blacks and whites. Known as the King of Swing, Goodman became hugely popular at the end of the Depression and paved the way for later bands—both black and white bands, as well as racially mixed ensembles like his own.

Two African-American bandleaders are generally considered to be the most influential among all jazz musicians of this era: Duke Ellington and Count Basie. Washington, D.C. native Edward Kennedy Ellington was born in 1899 to a creatively inclined, middle-class family and given a thorough educational grounding in music and art. As a teenager he was

The bandleader and pianist Duke Ellington was an adept composer, authoring over 2,000 musical pieces alone. His New York band, one of the most progressive and innovative of the American big bands, operated for nearly 50 years with a cast of talented sidemen who became well-known players themselves.

a talented painter and might have pursued visual arts if he hadn't already become an aspiring pianist and composer. Veteran jazz journalist Gary Giddins has reported that Ellington's first composition,

"Soda Fountain Rag," written at 14 and never recorded by him, was much indebted to James P. Johnson's "Carolina Shout," which, like many aspiring pianists of his generation, Ellington taught himself to play by slowing down the role on the family pianola [player-piano] and placing his fingers on the depressed keys.

This very motivated, handsome, and dignified young man eventually grew up, moved to New York, and became a world-famous performer. He was a genius at both composition and bandleading itself—one of his greatest talents was his ability to mentor and manage dozens of brilliant fellow musicians. In his arrangements, Ellington wrote parts not simply for "saxophone" or "trumpet," but ones suited to the individual personalities, playing styles, and sonic quirks of each musician in his employ. He was a born leader.

The creator of over 2,000 pieces of music, "Ellington is often called America's greatest composer," Giddins writes, "and just as often ignored entirely in discussions of American music, an indication of a [racial] separatism that continues to vex the nation's cultural habits." Many of his compositions are beloved jazz standards, played and recorded again and again by new generations of traditional instrumentalists and singers: "Mood Indigo," "Solitude," "I'm Beginning to See the Light," "Cottontail," "Prelude to a Kiss," and many others. Ellington was also responsible for sponsoring great compositions by several of his band members, such as trombonist Juan Tizol ("Caravan" and "Perdido") and pianist and staff composer Billy Strayhorn ("Lush Life" and "Take the A Train").

Ellington took his music very seriously and expected audiences and critics to do the same. For this reason, he was ambivalent about the label "jazz," which was still being used by cultural snobs to set this music apart from what they considered true art—and by racists to signify "primitive" music. "*Jazz* is only a word and has no meaning," Ellington once said. "I don't know how such great [musical] extremes as now exists can be contained under one heading."

Still, as Giddins points out, Ellington's music "is entirely rooted in what we recognize as jazz principles and usually (but by no means always) exhibits some or all of the standard characteristics: an equation of composition and improvisation, robust rhythms, dance band instrumentation, blues and song frameworks, blues tonality." Gridley notes that Ellington's New York band, which ultimately operated for nearly 50 years, featured a huge number of different themes, rhythmic figures, and chord voicings, making it arguably the most innovative and progressive of any American big band ever. In addition, many Ellington sidemen went on to become the most creative, original artists on their instruments: Cootie Williams, a trumpeter who pioneered the growl style of modern jazz trumpet playing; bassist Jimmy Blanton, who became one of the first virtuoso improvisers on his instrument and revolutionized the role of the string bass in jazz; Johnny Hodges, the lead alto saxophonist who perfected the technique of smearing, or *portamento*, which involves gliding from one note to the next "so gradually and smoothly that it sounds almost as if his instrument were equipped with a slide, like a trombone," in Gridley's words.

While Duke Ellington's band was setting the gold standard of New York jazz big bands, Count Basie was helping define the so-called Kansas City style of swing. William Basie, born in Red Bank, New Jersey, in 1904, ultimately spent 55 years recording music, 48 of those at the helm of his own orchestra. To this day, many jazz fans consider Basie's outfit to be the most swinging and consistently exciting of all the hot bands.

"Kansas City style was not based on the interweaving lines of the collectively improvised New Orleans style," writes Gridley. "Arrangements in the style were based instead on short musical phrases called riffs that are repeated again and again. Riffs serve

Bandleader Count Basie helped forge Kansas City-style swing. Many jazz enthusiasts consider his band to have been the most swinging and consistently exciting of all the "hot" bands. Basie's light and precise approach to the piano was very influential as well.

two functions. Sometimes they are theme statements, and sometimes they are backgrounds for improvised solos. A few of these riffs were written down, but many were created spontaneously during a performance ('off the top of someone's head'), learned by ear, and kept in the heads of the players."

Basie's band possessed an excellent sense of tempo and swing and generated an effervescent, buoyant feeling in its music. According to Giddins, the famed bandleader once explained his concept as follows:

> I've always built my band from the rhythm section to the [tenor saxophones], then onto the rest, for the living pulse of band is naturally the rhythm section. The piano can create a mood but it can also join forces with the guitar, bass, and drums to become a power unit that drives and motivate the entire outfit. The result should be "solid" but also flexible; there must be control that is not confined.

Like Ellington, Basie had an eye for talented band members; many of the best jazz trumpeters and saxophonists of this era spent time in his organization. The brilliant Lester Young, whose cool, fresh, light-toned playing helped inspire an entire category known as "cool jazz" in the late 1950s and early 1960s, was just one of many notable Basie band members.

Count Basie was also influential as a pianist: his light, precise, elegant approach to comping (short for "accompanying") and soloing defined a whole new sound for this instrument in the jazz context. Several other musicians of the swing era expanded the role of the piano in both big band and small combo settings: Art Tatum (1910-1956), who had dazzling technical mastery over the instrument and an unparalleled ability to spontaneously change the harmonic elements of the song (i.e., make instant chord substitutions) while retaining the tune's basic structure and flavor; Teddy Wilson (1912-1986), whose playing was as dazzling as Tatum's but a bit more stream-lined; and Nat "King" Cole (1917-1965), whose excellent piano skills were ultimately overshadowed by his success as a popular singer. These musicians paved the way for later ones who would take the art of jazz piano to a level of refinement, sophistication, and breadth equal to or even greater than the great keyboard artists of the European classical tradition.

Mary Lou Williams was a pianist, composer, arranger and bandleader who began her career in earnest in the 1920s, wrote and arranged for Duke Ellington's band at one point, and continued playing and writing for many years. She was able to make the successful transition from swing to later jazz styles.

5

Forgotten Women

Before we move on to the new styles of jazz that emerged out of the swing era, we should take a look at one other way that the history of this music reflects the social, political, and ideological divisions of American society at large. You'll probably have noticed the absence of women's names in our discussion of the development of this music during the first 50 years of the 20th century. Indeed, if you go on to read other jazz histories, you'll find almost no mention of women musicians who were instrumentalists rather than vocalists. Lil Hardin (1903-1971), who played in King Oliver's band and eventually married Louis Armstrong, occasionally gets a mention, as does Mary Lou Williams, (1910-1981), a brilliant pianist and arranger who was one of the few musicians of either sex to keep up with jazz's stylistic changes from swing to bebop and beyond.

Up to a point, this is an accurate reflection of the genuine rarity of professional female musicians—or professional females in virtually any field—during this prefeminist time period. But by the 1930s and 1940s, there were women playing in professional swing bands, and in fact there were a number of all-female bands (or all-girl bands, as they were then called) that achieved a fairly high level of national fame and popularity. Unfortunately, most mainstream jazz histories make no mention of this fact. In the year 2000, historian Sherrie Tucker published a fascinating study called *Swing Shift: "All-Girl" Bands of the 1940s,* in which she reveals that there were hundreds of all-woman professional bands playing during the swing era—but that these women were ultimately forced to the margins of the male-dominated music business, overlooked entirely by record producers, and then, in effect, ignored by history.

Well-informed jazz aficionados and historically aware feminists may know of a few of these musical organizations, such as the ethnically diverse International Sweethearts of Rhythm and the all-black Prairie View Co-Eds. But during the course of her research, Tucker learned that *several thousand* such women musicians came of age during World War II, played in professional bands, joined local musicians' unions, drew wages, toured the country, and performed for paying audiences. While male musicians were recruited to fight the war, females found their job opportunities suddenly expanded. This phenomenon was a double-edged sword, according to Tucker, as it "created the illusion that all-female musicians—no matter how experienced or talented— were 'Swing Shift Maisies,' 1940s slang for the substitutes for the 'real' workers (or musicians) who were away in combat." Thus, when the war was over, male musicians and promoters took center stage again and all-girl bands found themselves on the outs, cultur- ally and economically. In her piece "Women In Jazz" on the website for the PBS television series *Jazz,* Tucker writes:

> Despite the common perception that women would become house- wives after World War II, women's presence in the labor force grew in the post-war years, though countless Rosie the Riveters were

channeled into so-called "pink collar" occupations. Accordingly, many women musicians moved into musical fields traditionally considered "appropriate" for women, such as music education or accompaniment. Some put down their horns and switched to piano or Hammond organ to take advantage of the continuing relative acceptance of women at the keyboard.

With a little bit of investigation, Tucker was able to find that many of these women were still alive at the end of the 20th century, and a few of them were still playing their instruments professionally into their late 80s and 90s.

The musician's life is never easy, but it was especially difficult for these women at midcentury. Bandleaders and musical promoters of the era expected a female instrumentalist not only to play her instrument well, but also to look great in a fancy gown and high heels while doing so. In some bands, how you looked mattered a lot more than whether you could play—a fact that only contributed to the belief that only men could play jazz well. A woman who played a traditionally "masculine" instrument, such as the saxophone or trombone, rather than a "feminine" one such as the piano, was liable to be thought of as a lesbian. Young, single female musicians who traveled were apt to have their sexual virtue questioned. The same critics who argued on behalf of racial equality among black and white musicians often had nothing good to say about their female counterparts. Women musicians were destined to be inferior because they were emotionally unstable, wrote one typically huffy correspondent in a 1938 edition of *Downbeat* magazine:

Women are better performers on strings and piano, which are essentially sympathetic instruments more in keeping with their temperament. They do NOT shine on wind instruments, however, nor do they make good percussionists. If more girl drummers had cradle rocking experience before their musical endeavors they might come closer to getting on the beat.

In a 1941 edition of the same magazine, another article-writer mocked the entire idea that women were capable of being fans of jazz music—or, indeed, that women were capable of anything beyond blatant romantic manipulation. He began his piece by saying:

> There are two kinds of women, those who don't like jazz music and admit they don't, and those who don't like jazz music but say they do. The latter always have ulterior motives. They are either shining up to a man who likes his music hot, or else they're married to a hot musician and hate to admit to their friends that they have married a musical "failure." Any normal healthy woman can listen to music with you, dig your reaction before you're sure of it yourself, and beat you to your own comments on it . . .

These kinds of provocations, of course, played on people's endless fascination with the so-called battle of the sexes, and certainly helped *Downbeat* magazine sell lots of copies. But outright discrimination against women musicians was real, and so real women musicians occasionally made a point to speak up on their own behalf.

In one issue of the magazine, bandleader and saxophone player Peggy Gilbert got a chance to rebut some of the arguments made against women musicians, first by asking whether there was any evidence at all of their alleged inferiority in the first place. "Men have always refused to work with girls, thus not giving them the opportunity to prove their equality. This is especially true of wind instrument players." Gilbert went on to say that if female players were, in fact, musically weaker, perhaps this was a simple result of being expected to "smile with a horn in your mouth" or to negotiate difficult musical tasks "when a girdle is throttling you and the left brassiere strap holds your arm in a vise." She continued:

Pianist Lil Hardin played with King Oliver's Creole Jazz Band, as well as arranging and composing for other "hot" New Orleans bands. She met Louis Armstrong (fourth from left) and they married in 1924.

You say that women musicians are inferior because of lack of practice. If that's true, it's because there is no [professional] future in music for girl musicians. . . . Woodshedding [practicing] would be fun if we could see there was anything to be gained by it—other than personal gratification.

Sixty years after these debates in the pages of *Downbeat,* and after the upheavals and transformations of the feminist movement in the late 1960s and 1970s, it seems that much has changed about women's place in all sectors of American society. Some formerly male-dominated professions—accounting or law, for example—have experienced such a radical shift that there are now more women than men practicing them, while other persistently masculine fields—even "macho" ones like construction work—have become at least somewhat more welcoming to female practitioners.

But in jazz, as in these other fields, we still live with the legacy of the previous generations' cultural habit of excluding or marginalizing women. Though women in all musical genres are now recording, leading bands, composing for small combos and large orchestras, and occasionally achieving fame and recognition among fans and peers, they are still a stark minority. Female instrumentalists are still far more rare in jazz than their vocalist counterparts; indeed, judging from magazines and websites, there is still a strong cultural assumption that the phrase "women in jazz" automatically refers to the great divas of song, the Ella Fitzgeralds of yesterday and the Jane Monheits of today.

And while suggestions of the "innate" inadequacy of female jazz players may seem hopelessly outdated at the dawn of the 21st century, some observers note that discriminatory assumptions still exist. In "Women In Jazz," Tucker notes the persistence of the fundamentally sexist question:

Can women play jazz? While this controversy may seem hopelessly outdated in an era of such commanding female jazz performers as saxophonists Claire Daly, Fostina Dixon, and Jane Ira Bloom, and drummers Terri Lyne Carrington and Sylvia Cuenca, its effects linger like a haunting refrain. Women who play the saxophone, brass instruments, bass, or drums still encounter befuddled reception to their very presence: "I've never seen a woman do that!" or the ubiquitous, "You play good for a girl!" or "You play like a man!"

In another article published in *Jazz Times* magazine in September 2001, author and professor Angela Davis humorously subverts the whole notion that jazz musicians are, by definition, male. "Legitimate women musicians are described almost always as playing as well as a man. And I always wonder, 'Who is this man?' Any man?"

Perhaps the assumption that women are not suited to jazz will eventually become as outdated as the assumption that women are not suited to medicine, law, police work, professional soccer, or any of the other hundreds of pursuits that were once closed to them. In the past 20 years or so, jazz has become institutionalized as a part of the American educational system. Jazz bands exist in many high school and college programs, and more and more universities offer a jazz performance concentration as part of their formalized music major. Now that law and custom no longer bar young girls from such educational opportunities, observers have noted a slow but steady increase in the number of young female instrumentalists choosing to pursue a life in jazz. By the time they reach adulthood and artistic maturity, perhaps these women will be judged not as "female musicians" but as musicians, period.

Trumpeter John Birks "Dizzy" Gillespie was one of the foremost figures in bebop, a style of jazz that is regarded as the beginning of modern jazz—and is often reviled by fans of swing.

6

Bebop
"Outsiders"

Traditional jazz histories offer a smooth, organic narrative from one musical style to the next, with Dixieland setting the stage for Swing, which in turn set the stage for Bebop. While this is not an entirely inaccurate representation of the way one artistic style gives birth to another, some contemporary historians—or rather, *historiographers*, scholars who take a step back to examine the working methods and philosophical assumptions of traditional historians—question the cohesiveness of the traditional storyline of jazz. For example, Scott DeVeaux, author of *The Birth of Bebop: A Social and Musical History*, notes that

> any historical narrative as sweeping as the line that links the [protojazz] of New Orleans with avant-garde experimentation [of later periods] is necessarily vulnerable to fragmentation. Such a narrative links [musical styles] that are radically different in musical techniques and

social circumstances, while excluding other [styles] on constantly shifting and emotionally charged grounds. Its forging has been a noisy process, characterized by bitter disputes pitting advocates of one vision of jazz against another.

DeVeaux's point here is related to a fact we noted in our first chapter: that the very definition of "real" jazz is constantly undergoing debate and revision. For some people, for example, the development of a style of music called bebop (or bop) near the mid-20th century signaled the death of jazz. For other observers—those who were alive during this period as well as later generations of jazz fans and musicians—bebop was and is the *very beginning* of modern jazz. (And, as we shall see in our very last chapter, some of these hardcore bebop fans in turn believe that 1960s-style jazz fusion or 1970s-style "free jazz" marked the death of jazz . . . while others see those styles as the *very beginning* of a renewed jazz tradition!) It is not possible for us to explore these definitional and "metahistorical" debates in a very full sense. We should simply keep in mind that the following storyline—a fairly traditional view of how bebop emerged from the swing era—is only one of many ways to tell the tale.

"During the 1940s," writes Gridley, "a number of adventure-some musicians showed the effects of studying the advanced swing era styles of saxophonists Coleman Hawkins and Lester Young, pianists Art Tatum and Nat Cole, trumpeter Roy Eldridge, guitarist Charlie Christian, and the Count Basie rhythm section." Hawkins in particular had pioneered the use of unusual or unexpected note choices while playing solos over standard chord progressions in familiar tunes. Younger musicians, especially alto saxophonist Charlie Parker (1920-1955) and trumpeter John Birks "Dizzy" Gillespie (1917-1993), took Hawkins' lead and began experimenting with burning fast tempos (which were impossible to dance to!), daring note choices, unexpected rhythmic accents on weak beats (essentially, a new style of syncopation), highly detailed, unusually long phrases in both their melody-writing and their improvising, and dazzling, virtuoso-level instrumental techniques.

"Bird" (Parker's nickname) and "Diz"—along with many others both remembered and forgotten by music history—grew up playing mainstream swing music and apprenticed with some of the era's greatest professional dance bands based in New York. But in the hours after gigs, these musicians would attend open "jam" sessions in the after-hours clubs of Harlem (such as the famous Minton's Playhouse), establishments that stayed open until dawn and were frequented, at first, only by other musicians and a few hardcore revelers and music fans. The late-night jam sessions often took the form "cutting contests," in which young musicians were expected to prove themselves and to compete with one another. In such a macho, highly energized atmosphere, these young players burnished their technique and pushed the envelope of speed and dexterity. This leads one historian to wonder, "Who knows what modern jazz would have sounded like without this persistent desire for one-upmanship?" Yet at the same time, such an atmosphere also set the stage for inevitable collaborations and mutual influence, whether intentional or not. One musician's individual spark of "genius" might be quickly assimilated or reinterpreted by other musicians.

While Charlie Parker was still a young man playing in his hometown of Kansas City, he had an intuitive idea of a "new sound" that he wanted to play, a music that he could hear inside himself but couldn't yet play. In the hothouse atmosphere of the New York clubs, legend has it, Bird had an epiphany—a sudden moment of "enlightenment"—and realized that it was possible to use *any* note against any chord, as long as the player placed it in the right context. There was, in other words, no such thing as a "wrong" note. Parker was not the only one to arrive at the same or a similar conclusion around the same time, but for a number of reasons, he became the most influential. Soon

Saxophonist Charlie "Bird" Parker espoused the notion that there were no "wrong" notes in improvisation, as long as a note was placed in the right context.

enough, Bird's startling insight was common practice among all the beboppers.

Although horn players are most profoundly associated with the sound of bebop, other instrumentalists contributed greatly to the new style. In *Jazz for Beginners*, David cites drummer Kenny Clarke, who was "inspired by the work of Count Basie's Jo Jones" and who "wanted to create more tension in the music by setting contrasting rhythms against each other." Clarke and another drummer, Max Roach, were pioneers in expanding the drum's role beyond merely keeping the beat. They began including spontaneous "kicks" and "hits" between accented beats, as well as an ongoing, polyrhythmic "chatter" of pops and cymbal crashes. These techniques added a new level of energy, a new color dimension, to the music.

Pianists of this era also stretched the boundaries of their traditional role. Bud Powell used horn-like right-hand lines, borrowing the licks and phrases of Bird and Diz, while lightening up the role of his left hand: instead of playing thick, full chords on every beat in the stride tradition, he reduced his voicings to just two or three notes that suggested the flavor of the chord, and played them in short, spontaneous, syncopated bursts as a kind of counter-rhythm to the tune's melody or the soloist's improvised line. Pianist and iconoclastic composer Thelonious Monk suggested another pathway for modern jazz piano, making use of unorthodox chord progressions, odd accents, and jaggedly contoured lines. Like Count Basie, both Powell and Monk were minimalists in comparison to the earlier generation of strictly "timekeeping," space-filling swing pianists. Later innovators such as Bill Evans and Ahmad Jamal would continue the paring-away or process of simplification begun by their bebop predecessors.

For this period of jazz experimentation as in previous ones, it is difficult to unravel the cultural "roots" of these new developments or to separate "African" from "European" influences. Parker and Gillespie were both fans of European classical music, and to some great extent, their expanded harmonic conception was fed by their exposure to the musical "vocabularies" of composers such as Chopin and Debussy. Other aspects of bebop may have come quite simply from a natural yet mysterious process that takes place whenever musicians play together in environments where experimentation and innovation, along with imitation and competition, are broadly encouraged.

Bebop was, for the most part, highly unpopular among swing fans. It was fast, loud, furious, and completely unsuited for dancing. It did not easily accommodate singers. Unlike the flashy, well-choreographed stage shows of the big-name swing bands, bebop had no crowd-pleasing visual element: it was strictly for the ears. A writer in *Downbeat* in 1949 probably spoke for many bewildered listeners (and for many of jazz's non-fans today!) when he said that bebop

> has carried frantic jazz to the ultimate. In its feverish search for the superkick, it has entered a blind alley. Bop gives itself away. It considerable reliance on faster tempos, higher registers, and more notes per part is in itself a strong indication of insecurity and over-compensation. The more frantic jazz gets...the more it frustrates itself to the listener.

Bebop's initial unpopularity lends credence to the traditional view that Bird, Diz, and the others were rebels or revolutionaries. Some accounts romanticize the beboppers as heroes of race and class, African-American musicians rescuing African-American music from the watered-down, mass-market context of popular dance music. By other accounts, they were the first true modernists of American music, boldly defying commercialization, playing music for music's sake, in the same way as abstract impressionists were making art for art's sake. As writer and musician Ted Gioia, author of *The History of Jazz*, sees it:

Outsiders even within the jazz world, the modern jazz players had the dubious distinction of belonging to an underclass within underclass. Remember, this was a musical revolution made, first and foremost, by sidemen, not stars. Not by Benny Goodman, but by his guitarist Charlie Christian. Not by Duke Ellington, but by his bassist Jimmy Blanton. Not by Earl Hines, but by his saxophonist Charlie Parker.

But the musicians at the forefront of bop did not necessarily see themselves as musical anarchists. In his 1979 autobiography, Dizzy Gillespie rejected the image of bebop as an intentional attempt to destroy pop, blues, swing, or old-time Dixieland music: "It's true, melodically, harmonically, and rhythmically, we found most pop music too bland and mechanically unexciting to suit our tastes. But we didn't intend to destroy it—we simply built on top of it by substituting our own melodies, harmonies, and rhythms."

Here we come to a point where it's easier to understand what the historian DeVeaux meant by the term "fragmentation." If you are a fan of modern jazz, or player who has been steeped in the bebop tradition, you will look at this era in a much different way that if you are a fan of Dixieland or swing. Although big band music did eventually die out, it continued to be popular among large numbers of Americans through the 1940s, 1950s, 1960s, and even later decades to some extent. Traditional Dixieland music has gone through periods of waxing and waning popularity, and in fact, some observers believe that bebop's unpopularity helped cause a backlash that ensured a revival of Dixieland. Even today, if you go to New Orleans and attend something called a "jazz" concert, you may very well hear Dixieland, not swing or bebop.

As for swing, it can be reasonably argued that what killed the era of big bands wasn't bebop so much as the advent of rock and roll, as well as the ever-changing economics and technological capabilities of the music industry. (Why, for example,

Bebop infuriated or bewildered certain elements of the jazz community, and it inspired much discussion as to its merits and intentions. Here, Dizzy Gillespie is shown illustrating a musical phrase of bebop on a chalkboard in 1947, in an attempt to explain its mysteries.

would you hire a 15-piece band when a bassist, drummer, and a few guys on synthesizer and guitar can create just as full a sound? Or why bother hiring any live musicians at all, when a single producer can create a full orchestra using computer technology?) Meanwhile, swing continues to attract fans and followers in small pockets across the world, especially in Europe. If you go to London and attend a "jazz concert," for example, you may very well hear swing, not bebop or any more recent style.

These complications aside, it is undeniable that bebop was

a stylistic outgrowth of swing music. It is also fascinating to note that, for a host of reasons too complicated to discuss here, the "revolutionary" style pioneered by Bird, Diz, and the others has become the so-called "common practice" style of up-and-coming jazz musicians everywhere, in the same way that 18th- and 19th-century classical and romantic music comprise the common practice style of contemporary orchestral musicians. Nearly all apprentice jazzers are expected to know their way around Charlie Parker's tunes and solos, Bud Powell's chords, and Thelonious Monk's harmonies. But this definitely does *not* mean that bebop is the final answer to the question "What is jazz?"

Billie Holiday, or "Lady Day" as she was also known, was one of the few singers whose unique voice and interpretation of songs was revered by jazz musicians and fans of instrumental jazz.

Canaries and Cats

As we have noted, a large part of the popularity of swing music probably had to do with the inherent appeal of big band vocalists and the familiar pop tunes they covered. Although some fans were excited by the purely instrumental aspects of this music—and particularly, the quickly developing art of improvised solos—these, we presume, were a small percentage of the total audience for big band music. For these types of listeners, going to a big band performance often meant tolerating a "girl singer" (the "canary," in one of the colorfully sexist terms of the day) while waiting anxiously for the trumpeter or tenor player to get his chance for an eight- or 16-bar solo. With the bebop era, fans like these got their vindication. "Bebop was an instrumental music," writes author Will Friedwald in *Jazz Singing: America's Great Voices from Bessie Smith to Bebop and Beyond*:

No singer could have conceived it. Charlie Parker forever altered the fundamental relationship between voices and instruments as it existed up to that point. Horn players still had to breathe and so they had to base their phrases on the duration of the human breath, but no longer did they need to limit what they played to the boundaries of the voice. They played faster, way beyond what any human voice could articulate with clarity, and they played melodies that were never meant to be sung.

As a result of the primacy of instruments in bebop and later jazz styles, even today you'll find some musicians and fans who argue there is no such thing as a "jazz singer," only a "jazz-influenced" or "jazz-associated" one.

This snobbish dismissal ignores the fact that the relationship between vocal music and instrumental music—in jazz and, indeed, in all music—is a complicated symbiosis. It is believed, for example, that the early jazz horn players' preference for growls, buzzes, and other "rough" sounds bore some connection to ancient native African singing techniques that sought to achieve similar effects. Early 20th-century trumpeters, clarinetists, saxophonists, and trombonists consciously sought to imitate the scoops, tonal variations (e.g., "bent" or "blue" notes), and rhythmic conventions of classic blues singers, such as Bessie Smith. Meanwhile, the best vocalists absorbed styles and techniques from the great jazz instrumentalists who'd be hired to accompany them: a sense of swing, a jazz-like conception of rhythm and phrasing, and perhaps even a horn-like "timbre" or tone-color to the voice.

Some singers also took a cue from Louis Armstrong, the great popularizer of scatting. This technique involves using the voice to imitate the sound of a trumpet or saxophonist; typically, the singer uses nonsense syllables and sounds while creating a spontaneous solo in the same way an instrumentalist would. Ella Fitzgerald (1918-1996) was a master at this—and at everything else she did as a singer. She first achieved prominence in the

1930s as a member of the Chick Webb Band—an outfit for which she ultimately served as leader after Webb's death. She had her first hit in 1939 with a sassy version of *A-Tisket-A-Tasket* and continued to make hit records and concert recordings in her late 60s. Gridley writes that Fitzgerald

> is considered by many to be the most outstanding non-operatic singer of the 20th century. She had near-flawless technique. Listeners were impressed by her grace and lilt. Mastery of swing eighth notes and perfect timing of syncopations gave her singing the rhythmic effect achieved by the best swing era hornmen. Delivered with such bounce and lightness, her phrases actually swung more than those of some modern trumpeters and saxophonists.

Fitzgerald's contemporary Billie Holiday (1915-1959) is one of the few singers that even snobbish jazz musicians and instrumental jazz fans often openly revere. Holiday was nowhere near as technically accomplished as Fitzgerald, but she had a unique, horn-like timbre and a rare gift for dramatically interpreting a song. Friedwald contrasts the two singers as follows:

> Billie Holiday's art is the kind that takes you deeper inside yourself and ultimately out again; Ella Fitzgerald's is the kind that takes you outside yourself and ultimately in again.
>
> Holiday creates a five-senses reality out of the lyric to a song, yet her abilities as a musician equal or surpass any "pure" instrumental improviser to work in jazz . . . Fitzgerald makes melodies, whether a songwriter's or her own, soar through skies of aural heaven, and creates a no less effective, no less emotional kind of drama through purely musical means. . . .
>
> Both are capable of slapstick comedy and epic tragedy and all the gradations of feeling that fall between. Being true daughters of jazz, both can sing the blues, and both can swing—interpreting these foundation elements of the music no less personally than they do an individual song.

The slightly younger Sarah Vaughan (1924-1990) is one of the few jazz singers to have made the transition from swing to bop. Like Fitzgerald, she had a large following outside of the jazz audience, but gained the respect of many of the top jazz instrumentalists she recorded with, including Dizzy Gillespie. Vaughan was also a professional pianist and an accomplished scat singer, although she preferred to improvise with the original lyrics themselves, shifting the rhythms and embellishing the pitches, rather than creating a whole new nonsense-syllable solo. Gridley notes that

> Straight readings of tunes were not Vaughan's routine practice. She improvised extensively with the timing of words, as though the lyrics were elastic and could be stretched to occur almost anywhere in relation to the passing beats. At the same time she also played with the enunciation of the words and their tone's pitch and timbre. The effect is exceedingly sensual . . . Ballad performances account for her greatest achievements. The slow-paced tunes were excellent vehicles for her mastery of nuance.

Once bebop put instruments and especially horns at the center of the musical experience, the jazz vocal tradition moved along a parallel track, sometimes developing quite separately from instrumental jazz, other times more closely. Although the swing era has long passed us by, today there is still a strong tradition of singers, particularly female ones, who follow in the footsteps of Ella and Billie, cultivating the same elegant sort of performance style and revisiting a 50-year-old repertoire with (they hope) fresh interpretations.

Jazz in all its variations also had a profound effect upon pop music, whether audiences realized it or not. For example, Louis Armstrong was a major influence on Bing Crosby, one of the most widely beloved singers of the mid-century, whose mellow baritone voice and casual, conversational diction determined a new direction for popular vocalists.

Sarah Vaughan was one of the few singers who made the successful transition from swing to bop by making improvisation a key component of her interpretations of songs.

In one example of the persistent symbiosis between instrumentalists and vocalists, in the late 1940s, a former tap-dancer
named Eddie Jefferson helped popularize a singing technique
called "vocalese," the practice of writing lyrics to a famous horn
solo. "Instead of a wordless scat," writes Friedland, "Jefferson
. . . verbalized every note that [the original instrumentalist]
played, matching him inflection for inflection." This practice
became the basis for a new school of jazz singing, epitomized
best by the racially integrated, two-man, one-woman team of
(Dave) Lambert, (Jon) Hendricks, and (Annie) Ross. At the
end of the 20th century and beginning of the 21st, the art of
vocalese has been revived in a few corners of the jazz world,
most notably by singer/conductor Bobby McFerrin and singer
Kurt Elling (who is also a phenomenal scat singer).

But in general, contemporary jazz makes a great distinction
between vocal and instrumental music, and most self-described
"serious" jazz fans are still more interested in players than singers.
On rare occasion, a singular artist—such as the elegantly swinging pianist/singer Shirley Horn, or the eclectic artist Abbey
Lincoln—rises above the expectations of the "canary" (a dis-
missive label for the singer at the front of a big band) to be
respected as a genuine musician, a fellow "cat" (a term of respect
among jazz players).

Furthermore, with a few notable exceptions—such as Astrud
Gilberto's association with saxophonist Stan Getz during the
bossa nova craze of the 1960s, or Cassandra Wilson's work with
the M-Base collective in the late 1980s—singers have not been
close to the experimental, cutting edge of instrumental jazz.
Meanwhile, vocalists who revive old swing-era music continue
to draw the largest audiences in all jazz. Jane Monheit, for
example, has been hailed as the new Ella Fitzgerald, while
Diana Krall is crowned the successor of Nat "King" Cole, the
pianist/singer she has modeled herself after.

Once again, the question of what counts as "real jazz" arises
to complicate the issue of jazz vocalizing. For those nostalgic for

the swing era, who believe that jazz has gone nowhere but downhill from the mid-1950s, Monheit and Krall are truly "jazz singers" because they sing the old favorite songs in a recognizable style. For others who associate jazz with progressive developments in the art of instrumental soloing—those who listen to bebop and its later offspring—there may be no such thing as a true "jazz" singer today.

Drummer and bandleader Art Blakey was one of the pioneers of the "hard bop," a style that emerged in the 1950s and is still often heard today.

8

Bebop Backlash and Space Explorers

The typical bebop solo was (and still is) characterized by a flurry of licks, patterns, and arpeggios (broken chords) played at lightning speed. Higher, faster, louder—these were the qualities that many beboppers strived for. In the 1950s, two new "branches" of jazz emerged—one that can be seen as furthering but refining these bebop practices, and another that can be seen as a reaction against them.

The label "hard bop" (which has also been called post-bop, funky jazz, and soul jazz, among other labels) is used to refer to musicians such as pianist Horace Silver, tenor saxophonist Cannonball Adderly, drummer and bandleader Art Blakey, and trumpeter Clifford Brown. Musicians like these retained the hard-driving quality of classic bebop, but tended to add a funky, gospel-influenced, bluesy flavor to their compositions and to play somewhat simpler lines in their solos than Parker or Gillespie.

During this period, the role of the drummer expanded once again:

drummers like Blakey and "Philly" Joe Jones drastically minimized their timekeeping function and further explored the colorful, "conversational style" they learned from Max Roach. Hard bop was also the first stream of jazz in which composers tended to favor writing their own original chord progressions, rather than borrowing the melodies and/or harmonic structures of pop tunes. Charlie Parker, in contrast, wrote new melodies but based them on the chord changes of pop tunes; his "Ornithology," for example, is based on the old swing standard "How High the Moon." Over the years, jazz composers have written over 100 new tunes based on the challenging chord progression of George Gershwin's song "I Got Rhythm."

In sharp contrast with bebop and hard bop, so-called "cool jazz" aimed for a softer, slower, subtler, more relaxed mood. "Cool jazz" has often been characterized as a specifically white, West Coast style of music, but this view is a mischaracterization. Gridley notes that in reality, "the label has not been limited to the work of musicians who belong to any particular race or geographic region, and the California jazz scene of the 1950s had a number of different styles in addition to cool jazz." Gridley argues that although "cool jazz" had a number of features that separated it from classic bebop, "a substantial amount of music called 'cool' is not distinguishable from bop." Once again, labels need to be taken with a grain of salt.

Saxophonist Lester Young was one of the main inspirations for musicians like tenor player Stan Getz and alto player Lee Konitz, who forged styles quite different from Parker's. In *Visions of Jazz*, critic Giddins writes that Getz's playing was distinguished by an "undeniable lyricism . . . even at breakneck tempos" as well as the unusual sound he got from his horn, "a paradoxical blend of heavy and light." Konitz was (and, at the time of this writing, still is) also a virtuoso player; there are still people who argue that in speed, agility, and technique he was superior to Charlie Parker. (Debates like this often encroach upon a complicated minefield of racial politics, since Parker was black and Konitz is white.) Gridley describes Konitz's style as being almost completely unrelated to

Parker's, even at a time when most other young alto players were busy imitating Bird:

> Konitz played with a dry, airy tone that was soft in texture and light in weight. He employed a slow vibrato and preferred to use the alto saxophonist's high register instead of its deeper tones. His sound is the alto saxophone equivalent of Lester Young's sound on tenor. This was a historic departure from the warm, syrupy lushness of alto saxophonists Benny Carter and Johnny Hodges. It also departed from the biting, bittersweet sound of Charlie Parker. Also, Konitz was not inclined to sprinkle his improvisations with quotes from pop tunes as Parker did. Konitz also differed from Parker in rhythm and articulation, rarely using staccato...almost all his lines were legato and not percussive at all. The overall effect of the Konitz style typified "cool jazz."

Several other artists made significant contributions to the style known as "cool." Pianist, composer, and bandleader Lennie Tristano absorbed the language of swing and bebop but then forged his own style that included a substantial amount of "outside" playing—choosing notes that do not fall within the given chord structure—as well as collectively improvised "free jazz" that completely abandoned the traditional practice of using pre-arranged melodies, tempo, meter, or chord progressions. (Tristano, however, has never received as much recognition for his free jazz experiments as did later players like Ornette Coleman or Cecil Taylor.) "Cool" made its way into both small combos like Tristano's and larger bands. Pianist-arranger Stan Kenton (1912-1979) led the best known of the era's big bands, featuring classic bebop material as well as "cool" sounds.

Like Tristano, one-of-a-kind pianist Dave Brubeck forged a unique style of playing, composing, and arranging that almost completely avoids bebop melodic construction and rhythmic feeling. "He is unusually inventive and depends almost exclusively on original melodic lines, not the phrases that most of his contemporaries absorbed from the music of Charlie Parker, Dizzy Gillespie, and Bud Powell," Gridley writes. Brubeck was featured on a 1954 cover of *Time* magazine, a controversial event that upset many black musicians and fans, who couldn't help but notice that no African-American jazz player had ever been featured in the magazine. Brubeck later admitted he was deeply embarrassed by the racial implications of the situation, as well as by the sad fact that he was first shown the cover article by Duke Ellington—a musical genius who had never received such an honor himself.

As we mentioned in the last chapter, classic bebop is now considered the "common practice period" of modern jazz, the language that all up-and-comers are supposed to know. Hard bop is similarly mainstream. In contrast, "cool" is often relegated to a historical footnote. Yet to this day, performers like Brubeck and Konitz, and younger musicians influenced by them, continue to play concerts, embark on recording projects, and entertain loyal fans—once again proving that there is no single answer to the question, "What is jazz?"

In 1949, trumpeter Miles Davis—a bebop-trained player who would eventually forge many new styles and become jazz's most protean artist—and big-band arranger Gil Evans organized a 9-piece band to work on a recording project called "The Birth of The Cool." The music they created together had a lush, orchestral flavor to it, quite different from anything happening in mainstream jazz at the time. "Let us admit," notes Ron David in *Jazz for Beginners*, "that a few uptight jazz critics—guys who treat jazz like a temple you have to guard against invaders—consider the Miles Davis/Gil Evans collaborations mere elevator music."

Still one of the best known of all jazz musicians, Davis had a 50-year career in which he helped forge and promote several distinct styles of jazz. As a bandleader, composer, and improviser, he was a trendsetter for decades. At times, his fame as a musician was overshadowed by his drug problems, his taste for flashy clothes and cars, his multiple marriages and brutal treatment of the women in his life, and his sometimes outrageously racist

Trumpeter Miles Davis started out as a bebop player but ultimately forged many new styles of jazz. On the 1959 album *Kind of Blue*, Davis's restrained and subtle playing stood in stark contrast to the frenetic density of bebop.

comments to the press. Davis, a born provocateur, often made anti-white statements in public, yet he hired, collaborated with, and promoted white musicians, many of whom counted him as a friend. Like many old-time blues musicians and the rock-and-rollers they influenced, Davis sometimes seemed to cultivate his "bad boy" image. But the fact remains that he was one of jazz's most enduring and influential figures.

Writers have produced entire books to try to catalog Davis's musical achievements, but we can try to summarize them here. As a bandleader, Davis rivaled Ellington and Basie in his ability to hire and groom many of the most talented and influential players of the era. Lee Konitz, Sonny Rollins, Jackie McLean, Gerry Mulligan, John Coltrane, Wayne Shorter, and Joe Henderson were among the dozens of great saxophonists who worked with Davis, as did guitarists John McLaughlin, John Scofield, and Mike Stern. Davis also worked with great pianists such as Red Garland, Wynton Kelly, Bill Evans, Herbie Hancock, Chick Corea, and Keith Jarrett. Evans, Hancock, Corea, and Jarrett would go on to become the four most stylistically innovative and influential jazz pianists since Bud Powell.

As a composer and arranger, Davis pioneered or helped promote cool jazz in the 1950s, "modal jazz" in the 1960s, and jazz-rock fusion in the 1970s. And as a trumpet player, Davis created a unique, unmistakable sound, "so easily identifiable that we can instantly recognize that, even in the crowded mix of a rock record or the background music for a movie." In sharp contrast to the flashy, brilliant, loud, fast playing of Dizzy Gillespie and those he influenced, Davis favored a wispy, delicate, subtle tone—often achieved with the use of a muting device—and an extremely refined approach to soloing. "Davis is a master of self-restraint," Gridley writes. "His placement of silence is at least a significant as his choice of notes, and he often let several beats pass without playing. During the moment he is not sounding his own notes, the sound of base, drums, and piano comes through clearly, further enhancing the mood." Whereas the classic beboppers sought to fill every space of their solos with licks and phrases, Davis explored the possibility of creating musical excitement by leaving spaces empty.

In 1959, Davis recorded one of the most influential, beloved, and historically important albums in all jazz history: *Kind of Blue*.

In this record, Davis and his sidemen—tenor player Cannonball Adderly, alto player John Coltrane, pianists Bill Evans and Wynton Kelly, bassist Paul Chambers, and drummer Jimmy Cobb—created improvisations on the spot based on very simple, static chord progressions rather than the standard pop tunes jazz had traditionally used. This represented a stark and instantly popular departure from the frenetic activity of bebop; later, in the 1960s and 1970s, Davis would continue to develop his compositional style in this direction, favoring, according to Gridley, "tunes which did not have bridges, complex turnaround, or any section demarcations which can easily act as barriers to an unencumbered, free-flowing sound."

Around the same time, a saxophonist named Ornette Coleman was pursuing another alternative to bebop by experimenting with free improvisation, using no preset harmonies or chord progression at all. Because he worked without a pianist or guitarist, Coleman did not have to worry about clashing with another musician's chords, and was able to develop his music freely by following the internal logic of his melodic ideas, while the bassist and drummer followed along.

The "modal" and "free" approaches were highly popular among jazz musicians and fans through the 1960s and 1970s, even while more traditional, bebop-flavored musicians continued to compose and perform. Davis's space-oriented approach even influenced singers, such as the pianist/vocalist Shirley Horn, who learned from him a new, less crowded, less dramatic style of interpretation and phrasing. In the 1980s, much "new age" music was essentially derived from the jazz styles pioneered by players like Davis and Coleman. But for some bebop-oriented purists, these approaches represented the beginning of the end of "real" jazz.

Saxophonist John Coltrane was a hugely influential figure in the 1960s who went through a priod of infatuation with chord changes, even adding new ones in addition to the ones already present in a composition. Soon he would spawn a host of imitators as well as a journalistic debate as to whether he had caused the demise of jazz, or had given it new life.

9

'Trane
to Freedom

One prolific New York jazz critic had this to say about John Coltrane, the hugely influential and original jazz artist who came of age in the 1960s:

> ... Coltrane did not come to jazz from a tangential realm ... Though a late bloomer, he was a practiced, died-in-the-wool jazz player who apprenticed with Dizzy Gillespie and Johnny Hodges before making his name with Miles Davis and Thelonious Monk. When he began to attract attention, at age 30, he was not universally acclaimed. On the contrary, he was reproved for lacking originality (believe it or not), a sweet tone, and concision—never because he lacked authenticity.

In the 1940s and early 1950s, "'Trane" played tenor saxophone in an emotional, wailing style that was already somewhat distinctive. But by 1955, when he began working with Miles Davis, he had acquired a rough, biting, dark tone and remarkable speed. Later he also incorporated the alto and soprano saxophones into his work. Like Charlie Parker, Coltrane had a taste for fast, furious solos in which all spaces were filled with notes. He was also infatuated with chord changes, and in some of his tunes, he would add lots of additional chords to the ones already present in the original composition. Gridley writes:

> His system involved stacking distantly related chords on top of each other. Then, when he improvised solos, Coltrane devoured the chord changes, the fifth trying to acknowledge every note in every chord and every scale that might be compatible with it. This was a historically significant contribution to the evolution of jazz styles. Journalist Ira Gitler described Coltrane's furiously paced streams of notes as "sheets of sound."

In this spirit, Coltrane composed the tunes for his famous 1959 album *Giant Steps*, which featured rapidly changing chords and melodies with unexpected interval leaps. Several of the tunes from that recording, including "Countdown" and "Giant Steps," are still considered rites of passage for novice improvisers. Coltrane was, however, also an outstanding ballad interpreter; in slow pieces he "seemed to harness most of the energy he customarily released in his dense, multinoted passages and channel it into a few deep, full-bodied tones that seemed to glow."

Influenced by *Kind of Blue*, Coltrane also went through a modal period, represented best by his 1960 album *My Favorite Things* (which also helped launch the career of the brilliant Canadian-born pianist McCoy Tyner, still an active performer on today's jazz scene). Coltrane then began moving in the "free jazz" direction of Ornette Coleman, even recording an album with Coleman's usual backing musicians. By the mid-1960s, his early obsession with chord changes and scales was over; with his sidemen in the band, he seemed to have moved "through" this phase to a deeper approach that combined sustained piano chords, extremely slow harmonic progressions, long-repeating bass notes (called pedal points), and a more dramatic, rhapsodic melodic style on the saxophone.

Writes Gridley of Coltrane's immense reputation:

> John Coltrane exerted a striking effect on his listeners. People who hated his music fought in print with those who were impressed by it. Some felt jazz history ended with Coltrane, whereas today many feel it just started with him. Not long after Coltrane formed his own group, they were so many saxophonists imitating him the jazz journalists began complaining about a general lack of originality as vehemently as they had responded to the wave of Charlie Parker disciples who arose during the 1950s.

Coltrane has been the subject of much sociological observation and even spiritual speculation—especially because he was a reformed drug addict and a religious seeker who studied Far Eastern spiritual practices and spoke in divine terms about his own music. There is, in fact, a church in San Francisco named after him. Jazz writer Nat Hentoff once quoted a psychiatrist describing 'Trane's music: "It sounds like a man strapped down and finally screaming to be free."

Fans of avant-garde musician Ornette Coleman also tend to make the connection between free jazz, the tragedies of African-American history, and the struggle of contemporary black Americans still yearning for civil rights and justice—in a word, "freedom"—in an unequal society. As Gioia remarks in *The History of Jazz,*

> "Freedom" stood out as a politically charged word in American public discourse during the late 1950s and early 1960s—it would be hard, in fact, to find a term more explosive, more laden with depths of meaning, or proclaimed with more emotion during these tumultuous years...The word was imprinted on the public's

consciousness, dramatized in speeches by Dr. Martin Luther King, sung in hymns, brandished at Little Rock, Albany, Birmingham, Selma, and the other battlegrounds of the civil rights movement. It is impossible to comprehend the free jazz movement of the same years without understanding how it fed on this powerful cultural shift in American society. Its practitioners advocated much more than freedom from harmonic structures or compositional forms—although that too was an essential part of their vision of jazz. Many of them saw their music as inherently political.

While these generalizations about the era may be sturdy and accurate, however, it is always a complicated and risky business trying to "read" larger social themes into an individual artist's creative output. So we will not try to do so here. Instead, we'll take note of the fact that, whatever the politics of the day, the music played by Coltrane, Coleman, and other musicians of this era was genuinely radical and "freeing" on a purely aesthetic level.

A gentle, amiable personality, Coleman nonetheless had a revolutionary streak. His early albums were entitled things like *The Shape of Jazz to Come* and *Change of the Century.* Gridley notes that although his music is labeled free jazz, it

actually has quite a bit of self-imposed structure. Constant tempo is usually employed. Written and memorized tunes are usually used during some portion of his performance. Moreover, there is nothing haphazard about the freedoms with which he and his sidemen play. They are limited by their own decision to listen to each other carefully, and they plan their music while they improvise.

Other highly influential musicians of this period include: pianist/composer/bandleader Cecil Taylor, who according to Gridley "does not play with modern jazz swing feeling, and . . .

Composer, saxophonist, and violinist Ornette Coleman was a key figure in the "free jazz" movement, a style that polarized the jazz community. A fiercely independent figure who explored countless musical styles, Coleman taught himself to play the violin and even wrote for string quartets.

frequently emphasizes musical textures rather than musical lines"; trumpeter Don Cherry; flutist and alto sax player Eric Dolphy; bassist Charlie Haden; and tenor saxophonist Albert Ayler.

The 1960s and 1970s also saw the rise of very creative

ensembles that departed sharply from the bebop-associated "jam session" tradition of playing, in which the musicians would first state the melody in unison, then each take a turn creating a solo over the tune's structure. This is still the format that most live and recorded mainstream jazz performances use. Versatile bassist/composer/bandleader Charles Mingus instead relied on "the alternation of composed and improvised passages and on preset accompaniments," according to Gridley. Mingus wrote over 150 pieces and explored a huge variety of musical styles including gospel, blues, funk, bebop, Third Stream (a marriage of classical and jazz music), and free jazz.

Sun Ra was a pianist, arranger, bandleader, and true eccentric—he liked to claim he was born on the planet Saturn—who used a huge variety of sound sources in his pieces: African chants, tape loops, synthesizers, classical percussion instruments such as timpani and marimba, and brass or reed instruments not normally associated with jazz, such as piccolos, oboes, and bassoons. "Central to such work," writes Gridley, "is the notion that music can consist of sound by itself instead of sound in the conventional form of melody and harmony." The Art Ensemble of Chicago was one of jazz's most eclectic groups; Gridley notes that "many of their approaches have not been squarely within the jazz tradition." AEC performances included poetry recitations, dramatic sketches, costumes and make-up, free-jazz improvisations, and extended passages of silence along followed by sudden explosions in noise. It may not have been what most people considered "jazz," but it was definitely not boring.

These innovative players, composers, and bandleaders from the 1960s and 1970s were very brave and creative musicians, but their sounds have never appealed to a wide audience. "Not much modern jazz is played on the radio," Gridley writes, "but the situation is especially unfortunate for free jazz. Some major cities never heard more than a few samples of free jazz during the entire decade of the 1960s . . . the problem is that most listeners find [avant-garde styles to be] unswinging, harsh, and chaotic. So, ironically, this music of great innovation has received a very little exposure."

Trumpeter Maynard Ferguson led a traditional big band until the 1960s, when he moved away from swing and pursued a more fusion-like approach, often rearranging pop and rock songs.

10

Funky Fusions and Beyond

The 1970s ushered in some stylistic extensions to traditional jazz that became widely popular and ultimately managed to influence a great deal of mainstream, pop-music styles. "Fusion" is a label that potentially covers a broad variety of sounds that join (or "fuse") two distinct musical styles to create a hybrid; so-called Third Stream music, for example, can be seen as a fusion of jazz and classical. But in the context of this particular era, "fusion" most often refers to the specific intersection of jazz, rock, and funk.

Although those three styles share a common heritage in African-American folk music (e.g., blues and gospel) and continued to display some common elements, by the middle of the 20th century they had developed on distinctly separate tracks. In the 1970s, traditional jazz players such as Herbie Hancock, Chick Corea, Miles Davis, and John McLaughlin began experimenting with the kinds of rhythms, instrumentation, compositional approaches, and soloing styles found in rock and roll or African-American dance music such as R&B or soul. Writes Gridley:

> Drummers learned new timekeeping patterns [that] resembled those of R&B as well as Latin American styles . . . The rhythms were stated insistently, not in the jazz manner which regularly alternated tension with relaxation. The jazz-rock style maintained a high level of tension for long periods. There was considerably less bounce and lilt than in jazz of the 1950s . . . Pianists and guitarists often adopted repeating accompaniment riffs in place of the spontaneous comping that had been customary in jazz since the 1940s. Development of repeating patterns in a funk music style usually took higher priority than comping, though the more adventuresome accompanists played spontaneously and responsively.

One of the pivotal figures in this new hybrid was the Austrian-born pianist and composer Josef (Joe) Zawinul, who contributed compositions and arrangements to two classic Miles Davis fusion albums: *In A Silent Way* (1969) and *Bitches Brew* (1969). *Bitches Brew*, notes Gioia,

> legitimized a whole new area of exploration and experimentation for jazz musicians. This emerging rock-tinged sound substantially broadened the jazz audience. One suspects that it played a decisive role in spurring the improving financial environment for all jazz styles during the 1970s. Fans who were introduced to jazz through fusion soon developed a taste for other styles of improvised music.

Fusion generally involved a broadening of the "color palette" used by jazz musicians—in other words, a broadening of the range of acceptable instruments. Zawinul was the first pianist in jazz to regularly use synthesizers, as well as electric pianos such as the Wurlitzer (which he played in tenor player Cannonball

Adderly's 1966 live recording of Zawinul's tune "Mercy, Mercy, Mercy") and the Fender Rhodes. In 1971 Zawinul formed a jazz-rock fusion band called Weather Report, whose 1977 album *Heavy Weather* sold more than 500,000 copies, earning it "gold record" status. The album's signature piece was "Birdland," an infectious, highly danceable number that received a great deal of play on radios and at discos, and was later "covered" (rerecorded) by artists as diverse as the vocal group Manhattan Transfer and the big band led by trumpeter Maynard Ferguson. In its heyday, Weather Report boasted a number of extremely talented and significant musicians, including sax player Wayne Shorter and the brilliant bassist Jaco Pastorious. Pastorious was, according to Gioia, "a charismatic figure who dazzled audiences and introduced legions of rock fans to the intricacies of jazz. Who else could have inspired countless rock and jazz bassists to learn Charlie Parker's intricate 'Donna Lee' bop line on their instruments?"

One of Weather Report's most unusual aspects was its approach to collective improvisation on its first three albums. As Gridley explains,

> Instead of adhering to roles consistent with the bop traditions, the instruments in Weather Report performed a variety of different roles. Spurts of melody might come from any member, not just from the saxophone. Rhythmic figures and fills could come from any member, not just from a bassist or drummer.
>
> The kinds of interaction between members were so varied that in some pieces there was no distinction between soloist and accompaniment. One player's sound might stand out momentarily from the ensemble texture, but it soon blended into the overall texture again.

In the eyes of jazz aficionados, not all fusion experiments were born equal. In 1973, Herbie Hancock released a funky, electrified outing called *Headhunters*, which "achieved massive sales and attracted a following with a younger, urban black audience," Gioia writes. He goes on to contrast Hancock's experiments with his jazzier outings:

> This release initiated a bifurcated career for Hancock, with his efforts now divided between mainstream jazz, often of the highest quality, and overtly commercial projects with little jazz substance. His 1979 release *Feets Don't Fail Me Now* found him lamely singing (albeit with the aid of a voice synthesizer) and regurgitating a vapid pseudo-disco sound—yet around that same time, Hancock participated in a stunning two-piano concert tour with Chick Corea and an impressive reunion . . . of the mid-1960s [Miles] Davis quintet (with Freddie Hubbard filling Miles's role).

In mainstream music in the late 1970s and 1980s, a number of excellent bands absorbed lessons from jazz masters but retained a solid grounding in guitar-based rock and roll—Steely Dan, Frank Zappa, Chicago, and Earth, Wind & Fire, among others. On the jazz side of the equation, bands led by guitarists John McLaughlin (of the Mahavishnu Orchestra) and Pat Metheny captured large audiences without watering down their sound. (As of this writing in 2002, Metheny continues to be a highly active composer and player.) Trumpeter Maynard Ferguson led a traditional big band until the 1960s, when he moved away from swing and pursued a more fusion-like approach, often rearranging pop and rock songs.

But the initial excitement of jazz-rock fusion began to give way to what Gioia calls "an increasingly bland, formula-driven ambiance, as marked by the late 1970s and 1980s work of Spyro Gyra, the Yellowjackets, and the Rippingtons." In the mid-1980s, a group of young New York musicians calling themselves the M-Base Collective made another valiant attempt to mix jazz with popular dance-music styles such as funk and hip-hop; while their music was considered an aesthetic success

Pianist Herbie Hancock made several forays into fusion territory with his Headhunters project, among others. He even scored a Top-10 hit in the 1980s with the track "Rockit," which featured synthesizers, voice synthesizers, drum machines, and record scratching.

by many of their listeners, it never caught on with a broader audience. (M-Base did, however, help launch the careers of a number of still active, highly original jazz artists: pianist Geri Allen, vocalist Cassandra Wilson, and saxophonists Greg Osby and Steve Coleman.)

Out of the jazz-funk-rock moment, several new idioms of popular music emerged in the 1980s and 1990s, once again spurring questions about what counts as "real" jazz, or whether jazz had died entirely. The soft, smooth, wispy, background sounds of New Age music did not really come out of the jazz tradition—even when it incorporated elements of improvisation—but often got lumped together with jazz for marketing purposes. "Record stores initially did not have bins for displaying [this new style]," Gridley explains. "So clerks placed it in the jazz bins because they thought it sounded more like jazz than like classical music or rock. Even after this music earned a bin of its own, much of the public continued to call it jazz."

So-called "smooth jazz" became a popular radio format in the late 1980s and early 1990s. Quieter, less intense, and not the least bit adventurous, "smooth jazz" is considered by musicians to be an easy-listening style of background music: they have, according to Gridley, "dubbed it 'fuzak' because it is a jazz-rock fusion as soft and pleasant as the highly processed music that was once piped into office buildings's elevators, marketed by the Muzak company, informally termed 'elevator music.'" However much jazz purists complain about the insubstantial nature of this music, "smooth jazz" defines "jazz" for a great many listeners. In the mid-1980s, saxophonist Kenny G sold millions of copies of just one of his albums—exceeding all the recordings ever sold by Charlie Parker and John Coltrane combined.

"Acid jazz" had a brief moment of widespread popularity in the 1990s. The term was coined by British DJs to describe dance-party music created by electronically looping samples from classic jazz albums. It can thus be seen as a form of hip-hop or house music that simply makes use of jazz—and it was created by DJs and rap artists, not by musicians. As such, most jazz aficionados feel pretty safe in dismissing it out of hand as "not really jazz." But the label remains firmly stuck to the music.

The closer we get to our own time period, the harder it is to discern which forms of art, music, or literature will come to be seen as most significant by generations of the future. Bebop was not widely popular in its own time, but it has become the one style of music that nearly all aspiring jazz musicians feel they must be able to play, even if they hope to forge their own new sound, eventually. Meanwhile, jazz-rock fusion has seen its moment of glory come and go; despite its huge popularity at one time, it is still not considered a part of the necessary vocabulary of the "jazz tradition." Though it may seem permanent for the moment, this state of affairs is always subject to change.

Within any established art, there is a conservative force and a progressive force—a pull backward, and a push forward. At the end of the 20th century, it just so happens that the more conservative, traditional voices in mainstream jazz—for example, trumpeter Wynton Marsalis, who runs the jazz program for New York's world-famous Lincoln Center, or pianist Dr. Billy Taylor, who broadcasts a live jazz radio program from the Kennedy Center in Washington, D.C.—are primarily oriented toward bebop and swing. For traditionalists such as these, jazz is defined by a certain set of specific practices, sounds, conventions, vocabularies (e.g., certain standard musical licks and phrases), and compositional styles.

From this perspective, supporting jazz means retaining those practices, etc., from the previous generation and handing them down to the next generation. Marsalis, a brash character who was a youthful trumpet prodigy in both classical and jazz, has often publicly denounced any jazz past the mid-1960s. Taylor is a far more amiable, less strident public figure, but he thinks of jazz as "America's classical music" and narrowly defines the art of jazz improvisation as the creation of new melodies—in other words, the approach pioneered at jazz's very inception by men like Louis Armstrong and Bix Beiderbecke.

These conservative forces generally also want to keep a tight focus on the idea that jazz is, at its roots, an African-American music. At the same time, however, they are also characteristically uninterested or even quite hostile toward latter-day forms of jazz that seek to combine it with other forms of culturally black music—for example, go-go music, jazz-hip-hop fusion, or Latin jazz that combines Afro-Cuban dance music styles with jazz improvisation.

In contrast to these conservative voices, there are those who view jazz as an open-ended approach to music, rather than a certain set of sounds. From this perspective, jazz's most important features are improvisation—in the widest possible sense—and experimentation. Pat Metheny is called a jazz musician, but his music owes almost nothing to bebop; nor does his pianist and collaborator, Lyle Mays, who names Keith Jarrett as his main influence. The innovative pianist/composer/bandleader Myra Melford once confessed to an interviewer that she had never learned the standard bebop repertoire; from an early age, she was motivated to create her own sounds, her own unique music. Yet she is considered a jazz musician. Since the 1950s, musicians from Latin America have created a whole fresh, exciting set of sounds that owe something to their indigenous dance-music forms as well as to bebop and mainstream jazz improvisational styles. But in most jazz histories—including this one, unfortunately—Latin jazz is just barely mentioned.

There are also racial divisions in our society that continue to confuse or mislead us in cultural matters. The young piano-bass-drums trio of Medeski Martin & Wood, for example, freely combine jazz sounds with blues, gospel, and electrified funk—styles all rooted in black musical practices. They are some of the

Trumpter Wynton Marsalis is a purist who feels that jazz created after the mid-1960s has very little value—an example of one of the many viewpoints on the many styles of jazz music that exist today.

most progressive, forward-thinking musicians on the current scene, even while they retain a high sense of respect and awareness for past traditions. Much of their music involves electronic instruments and sounds like "techno" dance music—though it is generally more interesting and varied than that—but a good deal of their music "swings" in the traditional sense. Indeed, because they emphasize collective improvisation over individual solos, MM&W might even be considered the true "conservatives," going all the way back to the group-sound practices of Dixieland bands. But these three young white men, who spent their formative years plugging their music on the mostly white, rock-oriented "jam band" circuit, have made a much larger name for themselves outside the mainstream jazz community than inside it. Many jazz aficionados do not consider them "real" jazz—while many of their devoted listeners are primarily rock fans whose CD collections contain no other jazz.

Labels and categories are necessary to help us make our way through the maze of infinitely varied musical styles, but they will always confound us in the end. The issues of racial identity and authenticity that come up in jazz history are by no means unimportant or secondary, but ultimately they are separate from the music itself. Individual listeners should feel free to follow their ears, to listen to a wide variety of sounds and decide what they like based on the music alone—not on political or social considerations. One might love Miles Davis in his *Kind of Blue* period, but find *Bitches Brew* not worth the time, and that's perfectly OK. Or one might enjoy Herbie Hancock's funky *Headhunters* more than his modal work on *Maiden Voyage*, even if jazz snobs assert that the latter is a masterpiece and the former a musical mistake. It's also OK to consider oneself a jazz fan or jazz musician but not worship Charlie Parker, or to prefer instead the more angular sounds of his contemporary Lee Konitz. And it's perfectly fine if one only listens to jazz (or "jazz-associated") singers and can't stand the self-indulgent sound of a 20-chorus saxophone solo. One's choices don't have to be limited by labels. From the many outgrowths and mutations that have arisen from jazz over the years, there are many ways to enjoy this remarkable and diverse form of music.

1897 The New Orleans city councilman Sidney Story drafts a law that sections off a part of town as a red-light district for brothels and their customers—a move that inadvertently creates a market for nonstop musical entertainment and turns New Orleans into a hotbed of musical experimentation and development.

1900–20 As many black musicians joined their peers in the great migration north, the center of jazz slowly shifts from New Orleans to Chicago and New York.

1917 The Original Dixieland Jazz Band, an all-white group headed by cornet player Nick LaRocca, records the first jazz album in New York City. Soon thereafter in Chicago, groups led by trumpeter Joe Oliver and trombonist Kid Ory make what are now considered the first New Orleans-style combo jazz recordings by black musicians.

1922 White bandleader Paul Whiteman sells three million copies of his first recording of watered-down "symphonic jazz," while innovative black bandleaders like Fletcher Henderson, Duke Ellington, and Count Basie are busy revolutionizing big band music for a smaller but growing audience.

1927–28 Through recordings with his "Hot Five" and "Hot Seven" bands, Louis Armstrong introduces the world to his brilliant improvisational abilities and transforms jazz into a virtuoso soloist's medium.

1927–31 Duke Ellington reigns as bandleader during the most celebrated period in the history of Harlem's famed Cotton Club. He ultimately becomes one of America's most prolific and influential composers.

1935 Benny Goodman, a white clarinetist, achieves lasting fame playing black-style swing and leading an integrated band, playing mainly for newly receptive white audiences.

1940s Alto saxophonist Charlie Parker and trumpeter Dizzy Gillespie, two leading lights among young swing-era working musicians who develop bebop—a fast, frenetic, complex, virtuoso-driven music that polarizes jazz audiences into staunch defenders and detractors.

1949–1950 Trumpeter Miles Davis and arranger Gil Evans organize the nine-piece "Birth of the Cool" band; its subdued, understated style fosters the new "cool" school of jazz playing, later exemplified by clarinetist Lee Konitz, trumpeter Chet Baker, baritone saxophonist Gerry Mulligan, tenor saxophonist Stan Getz, and others.

1959 Miles Davis again positions himself at the vanguard of a new jazz style with his profoundly influential album *Kind of Blue*, which features a new, stripped-down, purified, "anti-bebop" concept of composition and collective and solo improvisation.

1960 Alto and soprano saxophonist John Coltrane records the album *My Favorite Things*, which set a new standard for so-called "modal" jazz; in later recordings, he goes on to develop highly complex and influential new ways of approaching jazz harmony, melody, and improvisation. Also in 1960, alto saxophonist Ornette Coleman releases his album *Free Jazz*, which explores the possibilities of open-ended, completely unplanned collective improvisation based on no preset song, harmonic progression, melody, or meter.

1970s Many leading jazz artists turn away from the traditional bebop-generated jazz styles—whether temporarily or permanently—to engage in various "fusion" projects. Piano prodigy Herbie Hancock releases a funk-influenced album called *Headhunters*, Miles Davis releases the controversial, rock-influenced recording *Bitches Brew*, saxophonist Wayne Shorter and pianist Joe Zawinul create the widely popular group Weather Report, and British guitarist John MacLaughlin forms the rock-jazz fusion group Mahavishnu Orchestra. Once again, the fusion movement helps splinter an already divided jazz audience into those who love it and those who hate it.

1990 Trumpeter Wynton Marsalis is featured on the cover of *Time* magazine with a headline proclaiming "The New Jazz Age." Marsalis has gone on to become one of the world's most famous jazz musicians and a puritanically staunch promoter of "traditional," pre-1960 jazz.

"Black, White and Beyond." *Jazz Times*, September 2001.

David, Ron. *Jazz For Beginners*. New York: Writers and Readers Publishing, Inc., 1995.

DeVeaux, Scott. *The Birth of Bebop: A Social and Musical History*. Berkeley and Los Angeles: University of California Press, 1997.

Friedwald, Will. *Jazz Singing: America's Great Voices from Bessie Smith to Bebop and Beyond*. New York: Da Capo Press, 1990.

Giddins, Gary. *Visions of Jazz: The First Century*. New York and Oxford: Oxford University Press, 1998.

Gioia, Ted. *The History of Jazz*. New York and Oxford: Oxford University Press, 1997.

Gridley, Mark C. *Jazz Styles: History and Analysis*. 7th ed. Upper Saddle River, NJ: Prentice-Hall, Inc., 2000.

Schuller, Gunther. *Early Jazz: Its Roots and Musical Development*. New York and Oxford: Oxford University Press, 1968 (reprint 1986).

Southern, Eileen. *The Music of Black Americans: A History*. 3rd ed. New York: W. W. Norton & Company, 1997.

Tucker, Sherrie. *Swing Shift: "All-Girl" Bands of the 1940s*. Durham and London: Duke University Press, 2000.

Walser, Robert, ed. *Keeping Time: Readings in Jazz History*. New York and Oxford: Oxford University Press, 1999.

David, Ron. *Jazz For Beginners.* New York: Writers and Readers Publishing, Inc., 1995.

Giddins, Gary. *Visions of Jazz: The First Century.* New York and Oxford: Oxford University Press, 1998.

Kernfeld, Barry. *What to Listen for in Jazz.* New Haven and London: Yale Unvirsity Press, 1995.

Roberts, John Storm. *Black Music of the Two Worlds: African, Caribbean, Latin, and African-American Traditions.* Second Edition. New York: Schirmer Books, 1998.

Shipton, Alyn. *A New History of Jazz.* London and New York: Continuum, 2001.

http://www.allaboutjazz.com/
[All About Jazz]

http://www.pbs.org/jazz/
[Ken Burns *Jazz* official site on PBS]

http://town.hall.org/Archives/radio/Kennedy/Taylor/
["What is Jazz?" audio lectures by Dr. Billy Taylor]

http://www.bbc.co.uk/music/jazz/
[BBC Music – Jazz]

http://www.bluenote.com
[Blue Note Records]

http://www.vervemusicgroup.com/verve/default.asp
[Verve Records]

page:

6:   ©Bettmann/Corbis
11: Hulton Archive/Getty Images
15: Hulton Archive/Getty Images
18: Hulton Archive/Getty Images
23: Hulton Archive/Getty Images
26: Hulton Archive/Getty Images
30: AP/Wide World Photos
34: ©Bettmann/Corbis
38: AP/Wide World Photos
41: ©Bettmann/Corbis
44: ©Bettmann/Corbis
49: ©Bettmann/Corbis

52: ©Bettmann/Corbis
56: ©Bettmann/Corbis
60: AP/Wide World Photos
62: ©Bradley Smith/Corbis
67: ©Joseph Schwartz Collection/Corbis
70: ©John Van Hasselt/Corbis Sygma
75: ©Lynn Goldsmith/Corbis
78: ©Mosaic Images/Corbis
83: ©Mosaic Images/Corbis
86: ©Bettmann/Corbis
91: ©Ressmeyer/Corbis
95: ©Lynn Goldsmith/Corbis

Cover: ©Bettmann/CORBIS
Frontis: AP/Wide World Photos

Sandy Asirvatham, a graduate of Columbia University with a B.A. in philosophy and economics and a M.F.A. in writing, is a freelance writer and jazz pianist/singer living in Baltimore. She has also written a history of the blues for Chelsea House, as well as several histories and biographies on non-musical subjects.